E
F
G
MR DAYDREAM
MR UPPITY
MR JELLY
MR SNOW
MR MUDDLE
MR GRUMPY
K
L
M
MR GREEDY
MR MEAN
MR NONSENSE
P
QR
S
T
MR SLOW
MR BOUNCE
MR SMALL
MR TOPSY TURVY
MR DIZZY
MR QUIET
X
Y
Z
MR CLEVER
MR WRONG
MR BUSY
MR RUSH

MR. MEN PICTURE DICTIONARY

Thurman Publishing

INTRODUCTION

Thousands of children have been captivated and entertained by the famous Mr. Men books. The characters created by Roger Hargreaves are instantly appealing and their popularity remains with each child for a considerable time. The books are returned to again and again, which confirms that the stories provide a most satisfying experience for children. The fun, the laughter, the mistakes and escapes, so dominant in all the Mr. Men books, have encouraged many children to read and enjoy reading.

This new and exciting MR. MEN PICTURE DICTIONARY has been compiled to encourage children further in developing reading skills. All the familiar characters appear throughout its pages, in lively illustrations that will stimulate and maintain interest in the dictionary. Very young children will discover that they can learn to 'read' the words because the pictures present accurate clues. For older children, the dictionary will provide endless opportunities to learn how to spell words they wish to write and to find out the meanings of unfamiliar words. Finally, by constantly using this delightful dictionary, children will quickly appreciate a sense of alphabetical order, which is a very important skill to master.

The MR. MEN PICTURE DICTIONARY is both simple and attractive, which ensures that children will enjoy using it and will learn so much from it.

Betty Root
Reading Consultant
University of Reading

Published by Thurman Publishing Limited
The Mill Trading Estate, Acton Lane, London NW10

Printed in Great Britain by
Purnell and Sons (Book Production) Ltd.,
Member of the BPCC Group, Paulton, Bristol

SBN 85985 171 0

Produced for Thurman Publishing by
Goodwin Dorman Publishing Limited
with Laurence Urdang Associates Limited

Educational Adviser Betty Root

able

To be able to do something means that you can do it. It is very useful to be able to read.

about

About means having something to do with. This book is about words. It is also about the Mr Men and some of the things they do.

About also means nearly. Mr Mean thought he had about 100 gold coins in his money box. When he counted them, he had 104.

above

Above means over or higher than. There is a picture of Mr Slow above Mr Lazy's bed.

above

absent

Absent means away or not being here. If you are ill, you may be absent from school.

absent-minded

Absent-minded means forgetful. Mr Forgetful is always absent-minded.

absolutely

Absolutely means completely. Mr Clumsy was absolutely soaked when he slipped and fell into the duckpond!

absurd

Absurd means silly or ridiculous.

accident

An accident is something that is not expected to happen. Mr Bump is always having accidents. He broke the kitchen window but he did not mean to.

ache

An ache is a pain. You may get a stomach ache if you eat too many apples.

across

Across means from one side to the other. Mr Topsy Turvy walked backwards across a zebra crossing.

across

act

To act is to do something. Acting also means playing a part. An actor or actress is a person who pretends to be someone else. You see them in films or in a play.

active

Active means doing a lot. Mr Busy is active from morning till night.

activity

An activity is something you do. At some schools, there are activities after lessons like playing games, making music, or learning about hobbies.

add

To add is to put one or several things with others. You can add sugar to tea to make it taste sweet. You can add numbers together. Mr Clever added two and two and made four. He was clever!

address

Your address is made up of the number or name of your house, and the name of the road and the town it is in. When you send a letter to someone, you write the address on the envelope. This tells the postman where to deliver the letter.

address

admire

To admire something is to think it is very good. Mr Happy admired Mr Uppity's car. He thought it was the best he had ever seen.

admit

To admit is to say that you have done something wrong. Mr Clumsy admitted that he had broken two of Mr Fussy's plates when he was washing up. He was rather sorry.

To admit also means to let in. Dogs are not usually admitted to shops that sell food.

adopt

To adopt means to take in as your own. Sometimes, people adopt other people's children and look after them as part of their own family.

adore

To adore means to like very much.

adult

An adult is a person who has grown up. Another name for an adult is a grown-up.

advantage

An advantage is something that is useful or helpful to you. It can be an advantage to be given a start in a running race.

adventure

An adventure is something exciting or dangerous. Mr Daydream and Jack went on an adventure to Africa. They were nearly eaten by a crocodile! But it was all right in the end.

advertise

To advertise something is to make it known. You can advertise something you want to sell or an event you want people to go to.

advise

To advise is to suggest to someone the best thing to do. The doctor advised Mr Bounce to wear heavy shoes to stop him bouncing all over the place. That was good advice!

Mr Small has been given an advantage in this race. He is starting in front of all the other runners.

aeroplane

aeroplane

An aeroplane is a machine that flies in the air and takes people to and from faraway places. Mr Rush likes travelling on aeroplanes because they go so fast.

afford

To afford is to have enough money to buy something. Mr Mean said he couldn't afford to buy any furniture. But he had a boxful of money hidden away, so he really could have afforded some.

afraid

Afraid means frightened. Mr Jelly is afraid of everything. The slightest noise makes him tremble and shake.

after

After means later than. Mr Strong feels stronger than ever after he has eaten a plateful of eggs.

afternoon

The afternoon is the part of the day between midday and evening.

afterwards

Afterwards means at a later time. A giant made Mr Greedy eat the most enormous meal he had ever seen. Mr Greedy felt very ill afterwards.

again

Again means once more. Mr Messy looked quite clean after he had a bath. But he soon got dirty again.

against

against

Against means touching. Mr Clumsy leant against a door that had just been painted, and he got paint all over his arm.

Against also means opposite to. Our football team plays against another one every Saturday.

age

The age of something is how old it is. Many children start school at the age of five.

ago

Ago means past or before now. Two hundred years ago there were no cars and no aeroplanes. The train left the station a minute ago.

agree

To agree with someone is to think in the same way. The people of Tiddletown all agreed that Mr Nosey was far too nosey for his own good.

ahead

Ahead means in front. When you are winning a race, you are ahead of all the others.

aim

To aim is to point towards something you are trying to hit. Mr Clever is aiming an arrow at the target.

aim

air

Air is what you take into your lungs when you breathe. It is all around but you cannot feel it or see it. You open a window to let fresh air into a stuffy room.

alarm

An alarm is a loud noise that warns people of danger. If the fire alarm rings in a building everyone must go outside, because the building might be on fire.

An alarm clock makes a noise that wakes you up in the morning. Mr Noisy's alarm clock is so loud, it wakes up everyone else in the town as well!

alarm

alike

Alike means much the same. Mr Skinny and Mr Greedy are not at all alike. Mr Skinny is very thin. Mr Greedy is very fat.

alive

Alive means living, not dead. Plants need water to stay alive. So do fish!

all

All means everything. If Mr Greedy eats all the sweets in this jar he will make himself ill.

allow

To allow means to let someone do something. I am allowed to watch television until eight o'clock.

almost

Almost means nearly. Mr Small can almost reach Mr Bounce's doorbell but he is not quite tall enough.

alone

Alone means on your own. Mr Chatterbox doesn't like being alone. When he is alone, he has no one to talk to.

along

Along means from one end to the other. There is a neat row of flowers growing along the edge of Mr Fussy's lawn.

aloud

Aloud means in a voice that can be heard. When you read a story aloud other people can hear you.

alphabet

The alphabet is all the 26 letters from A to Z.

already

Already means by this time. Mr Silly went to help Mr Busy paint his house. But Mr Busy had already finished when Mr Silly arrived. It only took Mr Busy five minutes to paint the whole house!

also

Also means as well. This book is about words. It is also about the Mr Men.

although

Although means in spite of something. Although he couldn't swim, Mr Tall went to the seaside with Mr Small.

altogether

Altogether means when every one or everything is counted. There are 39 Mr Men altogether.

always

Always means all the time. Mr Worry always has a problem of one kind or another. He never stops worrying.

amaze

To amaze is to surprise someone very much. Mr Nonsense was amazed to see Mr Impossible walking on the ceiling. He couldn't believe it!

ambulance

An ambulance is a type of vehicle used to take people who have been hurt or are ill to hospital.

among

Among means in the middle of. Mr Quiet's house is among the trees in the middle of a wood.

The wizard is taking a photograph of the Mr Men. There are 39 Mr Men altogether.

amphibian

amphibian

An amphibian is a cold-blooded animal that spends part of its life on land and part in the water. Frogs are amphibians.

amphibious

Amphibious means able to go as well in water as on land. An amphibious vehicle goes like a car on land and like a boat on water.

amuse

To amuse is to make someone laugh. Mr Silly was amused by Mr Funny when he pulled a funny face.

amuse

angry

Angry means very cross. Mr Fussy was angry with Mr Mischief for digging a hole in the lawn.

animal

An animal is any living creature that moves about. Birds, fish, insects, reptiles and mammals are all animals.

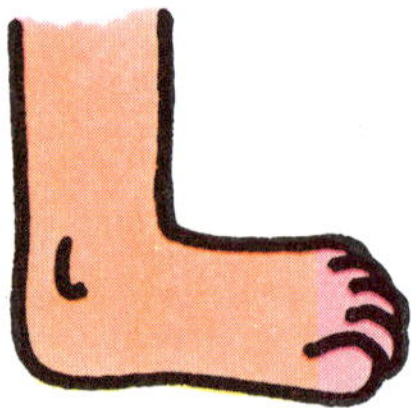

ankle

ankle

Your ankle is the part of your body between your foot and leg.

annoy

To annoy is to make someone cross. Mr Grumpy was annoyed to find flowers growing in his garden. He hates pretty things!

another

Another means one more. Mr Greedy is wondering whether he can find room for another cream cake. He has eaten four already!

answer

An answer is a reply to a question. Mr Happy asked Mr Topsy Turvy how he was feeling. Mr Topsy Turvy replied, "Thank you. Well very." What a funny answer!

anxious

Anxious means worried. Mr Worry was anxious when it rained because he thought his roof might leak. When it didn't rain, he was anxious that all the plants in his garden might die!

apart

Apart means away from each other. Mr Silly and Mr Nonsense do not live very far apart.

Apart also means into pieces. Mr Clumsy did not mean to break this chair. It just came apart in his hands!

apart

apologise

To apologise is to say sorry. Mr Grumpy did not apologise to Mr Happy for treading on his toe. He wasn't sorry at all. He did it on purpose!

appear

To appear means to come into sight. When a strange face appeared at Mr Jelly's window he hid under a chair, he was so frightened. But it was only Mr Mischief playing tricks as usual.

appetite

An appetite is a feeling of wanting to eat. Mr Strong has a very big appetite. He eats eggs for his breakfast, lunch and tea. Lots of them!

applaud

To applaud is to clap your hands to show that you like something. People applaud at the end of a concert or play.

apple

An apple is a round fruit that you can eat. Apples grow on trees and you pick them when they are ripe.

apple

approach

To approach something is to go near it.

approve

To approve of something is to be pleased with it. Mr Greedy approved of Mr Happy's idea to have a picnic in the park.

area

An area is a particular piece of land or water.

argue

To argue is to say that you do not agree with someone. Mr Silly and Mr Nonsense had an argument about what to have for dinner. Mr Nonsense wanted porridge pie and Mr Silly wanted apple stew. They argued for ages. In the end, they decided to have both. Porridge pie with apple stew!

arm

Your arm is the part of your body between your shoulder and your hand. Mr Tickle has got extraordinarily long arms.

army

An army is a large number of soldiers who fight together against an enemy.

around

Around means on all sides. Mr Bump has bandages around his head and his body.

arrange

To arrange is to put something in order. In this dictionary the words are arranged in alphabetical order.

To arrange also means to make plans for something. Mr Busy arranged to meet Mr Slow at six o'clock, but Mr Slow was late as usual.

arrest

To arrest is to take someone to the police station because he has done something wrong. Policemen arrest burglars and thieves.

arrive

To arrive is to reach somewhere. Mr Rush ran all the way to the station to catch his train. He arrived two hours early!

arrow

An arrow is a straight stick with a point at one end and feathers at the other. It is shot from a bow.

An arrow is also a sign that tells you which way to go.

artificial

Artificial means made by man. Real flowers die, but artificial flowers are made of plastic or paper and last for ever.

artist

An artist is a person who paints pictures or makes beautiful things.

ashamed

Ashamed means feeling upset and sorry because you have done something wrong. The wizard told Mr Mischief he ought to be ashamed of himself for playing tricks on everyone.

arrest

ask

To ask is to put a question to somebody. Mr Grumpy asked Mr Muddle how to get to the post office. But Mr Muddle told him the way to the station instead. Mr Grumpy was not very pleased!

asleep

Asleep means sleeping and not awake. Mr Lazy spends most of the day asleep.

assemble

To assemble is to come together. When Mr Bump got his hand stuck in a pillarbox, a crowd soon assembled to see what was going on.

assembly

An assembly is a gathering of people. Many schools have an assembly in the mornings, when all the children and teachers are together.

assistant

An assistant is a person who helps. A shop assistant helps you buy what you want and takes your money when you pay.

asthma

Asthma is an illness that makes it difficult for people to breathe.

astonish

To astonish means to surprise someone very much. Mr Happy was astonished to see Mr Strong lifting a tree with one hand.

attach

To attach something is to join it on to something else.

attack

attack

To attack means to start fighting. Mr Jelly thought he was going to be attacked by a man-eating snake. He was frightened. But it was only a friendly worm!

The teacher told the children some good news in assembly today.

attention

To pay attention is to listen or watch carefully. Your teacher expects you to pay attention during lessons.

audience

An audience is the group of people who listen to music or watch a play in a theatre or hall.

autumn

Autumn is the season that comes between summer and winter. In autumn some leaves turn brown and fall from the trees, the evenings get darker, and colder weather starts.

avoid

To avoid is to keep away from. Mr Bump stepped sideways to avoid a puddle. But he slipped instead and fell down.

awake

Awake means not asleep. Mr Lazy is nearly always asleep. He is not awake very often.

away

Away means not being there. Mr Nonsense called at Mr Silly's house on Tuesday but he was away. He had gone away for the weekend. On Tuesday! How silly!

Away also means far from. Mr Tall lives 40 miles away from the seaside but it takes him only four minutes to walk there, his legs are so long.

awful

Awful means very bad. Mr Messy's house is in an awful mess. The windows are broken and the paint is peeling and the garden is overgrown.

awkward

Awkward means difficult to manage. Mr Happy wanted to clean his bedroom carpet but his bed was awkward to move. So he asked Mr Strong to help him. Mr Strong didn't find it awkward.

axe

An axe is a tool used for chopping wood. It has a handle and a sharp metal blade at one end.

B b

back

The back of something is the part furthest away from the front. Mr Slow is at the back of the bus queue.

Your back is the part of your body that is behind you. You bend your back when you touch your toes.

back

bad

Bad means not good. Mr Mischief was punished by a wizard for his bad behaviour. He sawed through Mr Happy's chair legs. He sent Mr Greedy a cotton wool cake with toothpaste icing and he filled Mr Funny's hat with treacle. He was bad!

bag

A bag is used to carry things in. A shopping bag has handles and holds a lot of shopping.

bake

To bake is to cook food, like bread or cakes, in a hot oven. Mr Greedy can't be bothered to bake his own cakes. He buys them from the baker. The baker bakes bread and cakes.

backwards

If someone is moving backwards, he is moving with his back first. Mr Topsy Turvy sometimes walks backwards. When you go on a swing, you go backwards and forwards.

Mr Topsy Turvy sometimes walks down the street backwards. What a funny man!

Mr Noisy is leading the Wobbletown band.
He loves the loud noisy music.

balance

To balance is to stay steady and not fall over. To ride a bicycle you have to keep your balance.

bald

Bald means having no hair on the top of the head. Quite a lot of men go bald as they grow older.

ball

A ball is a round object for playing with. Balls are used in games like football and tennis. Balls are different sizes. A football is much bigger than a tennis ball. A golf ball is very small.

banana

A banana is a fruit. Bananas grow in bunches on trees in hot countries. They are long and soft and have a thick yellow skin. You must peel off the skin before you eat the fruit inside.

band

A band is a group of people who play musical instruments together. Pop groups form a band and play instruments like the guitar and the drums.

bandage

A bandage is a strip of clean white material. You put a bandage round a bad cut to keep it clean. Mr Bump is always covered in bandages because he keeps bumping into things and hurting himself.

bank

A bank is a piece of sloping ground. There are banks on both sides of a river.

Another kind of bank is a place where people put their money to keep it safe. Mr Uppity is very rich. He keeps all his money in a bank.

bare

Something that is bare has nothing on it. When you have a bath you take your clothes off and then you are bare. Many trees are bare in winter because their leaves have fallen off.

bark

To bark is to make the noise that a dog makes.

Bark also means the rough covering on the trunk and branches of a tree.

barn

A barn is a building on a farm. Farmers put hay in a barn to keep it dry.

barn

basin

A basin is a round dish. In the kitchen, basins are used to mix things in.

basket

A basket is used to carry or hold things. It is made of pieces of bent wood or straw woven together.

bat

bat

A bat is a wooden object with a handle. It is used to hit a ball. You play cricket and rounders with a bat.

Another kind of bat is a small flying mammal that flies at night. Bats have furry bodies and are like mice. Their wings are made of thin skin.

bath

A bath is a big tub that you can fill with water and sit in. When you have a bath, you can wash yourself all over. Mr Messy gets himself so dirty, he needs a bath every day.

bathe

To bathe is to go into the water. You can bathe at the seaside or at the swimming pool.

battered

Battered means knocked about. Mr Clumsy's suitcase is very battered because he has dropped it so many times.

battle

A battle is a fight between people, ships or aeroplanes.

beach

The beach is a strip of sand at the edge of the sea. Mr Happy went to the beach with his friends. They built sandcastles there and bathed in the sea.

beak

A beak is a bird's mouth. Beaks are hard and made of horn. Different birds have different-shaped beaks.

bean

A bean is a vegetable. Beans are the seeds and sometimes the seed pods of plants. Some beans that we can eat are runner beans, broad beans and French beans, but there are many others.

bear

A bear is a large heavy mammal with long fur and strong claws.

If you can't bear something, it means you don't like it. Mr Slow can't bear to be rushed.

To bear also means to hold something up or to carry it. If you climb a tree, you must make sure that the branches can bear your weight.

beard

A beard is the hair that grows on a man's chin and cheeks. Some men let their beards grow long, but others like to shave every day. Mr Fussy has a moustache, but he hasn't got a beard.

beat

To beat someone is to win. Mr Rush beat Mr Slow in a running race.

To beat also means to hit something over and over again. On a stormy day, the waves beat against the sea wall.

beautiful

Beautiful means lovely to look at. On a clear day there is a beautiful view from the top of the hill.

because

Because means for the reason that. Mr Small had to leave his job at the sweetshop because he kept falling into the jars of sweets.

bed

A bed is a piece of furniture that you sleep on. It has a soft mattress and pillows to make you comfortable. Mr Nonsense does not have a bed in his bedroom. He sleeps in a rowing boat!

bee

A bee is a black and yellow insect. Bees make a buzzing noise with their wings. They also make honey. They sometimes sting when they are annoyed.

bee

beer

Beer is a cold drink for grown-ups. It has a bitter taste.

beetle

A beetle is an insect with four wings. There are many different kinds of beetle. Their front wings make a hard case that protects the folded back wings.

before

Before means earlier than. Mr Forgetful forgot to put a stamp on his letter before he posted it. He remembered afterwards, but it was too late by then.

The dog had to beg Mr Mean for half a biscuit.

beg

To beg is to ask for something you want very much. When a dog begs for a biscuit he sits up on his back legs and raises his front paws.

begin

To begin means to start. Mr Lazy had just begun to mow his lawn when it began to rain. So he went back to bed instead!

behave

To behave well is to be good. To behave badly is to be naughty. Mr Mischief never behaves himself when he goes out to tea. He puts salt in the sugar bowl and pepper on the cakes. His behaviour is very bad.

behind

Behind means at the back of. Mr Nosey is hiding behind a tree.

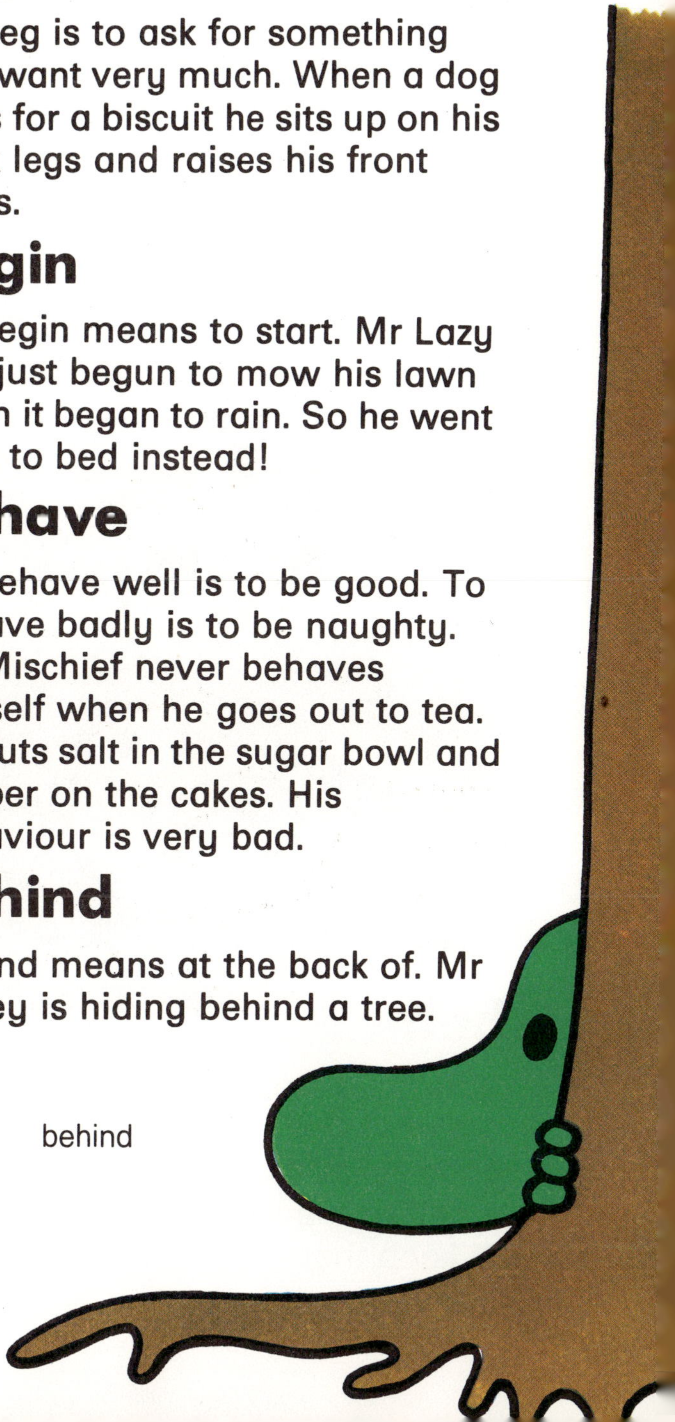

behind

believe

To believe something is to be sure that it is true. Not many people believe that ghosts exist.

bell

A bell is an object that makes a ringing sound. The conductor rings the bell on a bus to tell the driver to stop or start.

belong

Something that belongs to you is owned by you. Your clothes belong to you. They are yours.

below

Below means underneath or lower than. Pete Worm has made his home in the ground below Mr Small's house.

belt

A belt is a strip of leather or other material that you wear round your waist. Men sometimes wear a belt at the top of their trousers to keep them up.

Mr Tall had to bend his knees to talk to Mr Small.

bend

To bend is to be not straight. You bend your knees when you kneel down.

beside

Beside means next to. Mr Chatterbox sat beside Mr Quiet on the bus and chattered all the way to town.

besides

Besides means as well. When Mr Greedy had breakfast, he had a whole packet of cornflakes and a whole bowlful of sugar, besides three eggs and nine slices of toast!

between

Between means in the middle. Mr Clever is standing between Mr Wrong and Mr Grumpy.

bicycle

A bicycle is a machine that you ride on. It has two wheels and two pedals. You push the pedals with your feet to make the wheels go round.

big

Big means large. An elephant is a big animal. Mr Tall is much bigger than Mr Small.

bird

A bird is an animal that has feathers. Birds have two legs and two wings and most of them can fly. Their mouth is a hard beak. Sparrows and penguins and chickens are all birds.

birthday

Your birthday is the day on which you were born. Birthday cards and birthday presents are sent to people to celebrate this day each year.

birthday

biscuit

A biscuit is a hard flat cake. Some biscuits have chocolate on them. Those are the ones that Mr Greedy likes best.

bit

A bit is a small piece. Mr Fussy was annoyed to find a bit of mud on his carpet when he had just cleaned it.

bite

To bite something is to cut it with your teeth. Mr Greedy has taken a large bite out of the chocolate bar.

bite

black

Black is the darkest colour. The words on this page are printed in black ink.

blade

A blade is the sharp metal part of a knife.

A blade is also a leaf of grass. Mr Fussy likes to straighten out the blades of grass on his lawn after someone has walked on them.

blame

To blame someone for something is to say it is his fault. When Mr Happy's chair fell to pieces he blamed Mr Mischief.

blanket

A blanket is a soft warm cover for a bed. Mr Sneeze has to have lots of blankets on his bed because he lives in Coldland.

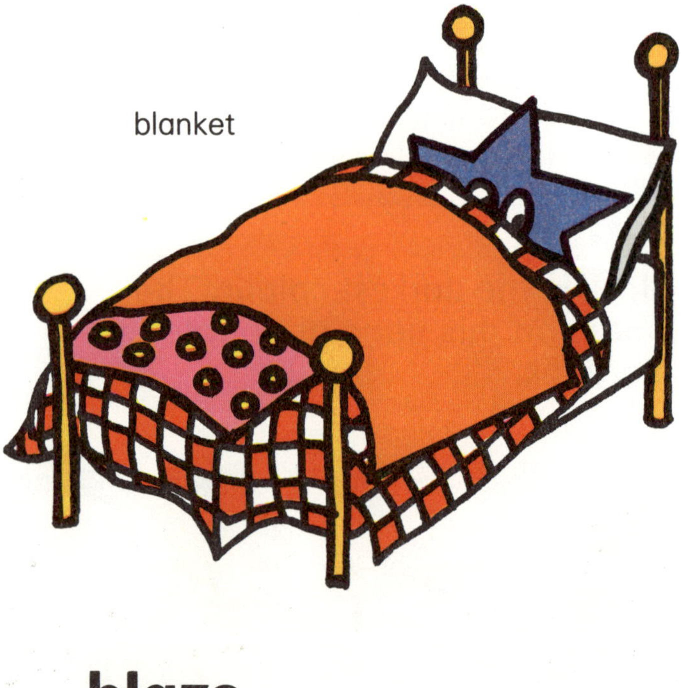

blanket

blaze

To blaze is to burn very brightly. A fire will blaze if you put dry twigs on it.

blind

Blind people cannot see because there is something wrong with their eyes. Sometimes they have guide dogs to help them find their way.

A blind is something that is used to cover a window to keep the sun out. Mr Grumpy hates sunshine. He always pulls the blinds down on a sunny day.

blink

To blink is to shut your eyes and open them again very quickly. A sudden flash of bright light may make you blink.

bliss

Bliss is feeling very happy.

block

To block means to get in the way. Mr Strong helped to move a fallen tree that was blocking the road.

A block is also a big lump of something like stone or wood.

block

blood

Blood is a red liquid that flows around inside your body. Mammals and birds have warm blood but reptiles and amphibians have cold blood.

blouse

A blouse is a kind of shirt that women and girls wear with a skirt or trousers.

blow

To blow is to push air out through the mouth or nose. When Mr Strong went to blow out the candles on his birthday cake, he blew the cake right out of the window!

A blow is a hard knock made with the fist.

A blow can also mean a nasty shock or disappointment. It can be a bad blow if you lose your pocket money.

blue

blue

Blue is the colour of the sky on a sunny day.

blunder

A blunder is a silly mistake. Mr Muddle is always making blunders.

blunt

Blunt means not sharp. It is hard to draw a thin line with a blunt pencil.

Blunt also means frank and direct. People who speak bluntly may seem rude.

blush

To blush is to go red in the face. People sometimes blush when they have done something silly, or when someone says something nice to them and they feel embarrassed or shy.

boast

To boast is to talk a lot about yourself and the things you can do. Mr Clever boasted that he was the Cleverest Person In The World. But he couldn't tell Mr Small how to grow bigger.

boat

A boat is used to travel on water. A rowing boat has oars to push it along. A sailing boat has a sail, which catches the wind.

Mr Silly and Mr Nonsense are trying to row a boat.

body

A body is all the parts of a person or an animal put together.

boil

To boil water is to make it very hot until it starts to bubble. To make tea you have to boil the water before you put it in the teapot.

bomb

A bomb is a hollow case filled with explosive. A bomb explodes when it is dropped.

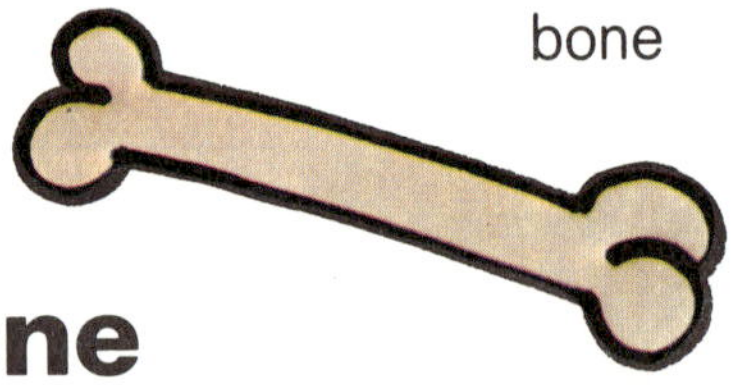
bone

bone

A bone is part of the body of a person or animal. Bones are hard and stiff.

book

A book is made up of pages fastened between two covers. You read a story book. You write in an exercise book.

boomerang

A boomerang is a flat piece of wood that is bent in the middle. If you throw it in a special way it will come back to you. Boomerangs were used in Australia by Aborigines for killing animals.

boot

A boot is a shoe that covers part of your leg as well as your foot. You wear boots in the rain and snow to keep your feet and legs dry.

A boot is also the part of a car where you put luggage.

bored

Bored means having nothing interesting to do. When Mr Tickle is bored he goes out looking for someone to tickle.

boring

Boring means not interesting. Mr Lazy fell asleep in the middle of a boring film.

born

To be born is to come into the world as a baby. Baby animals are quite weak when they have just been born.

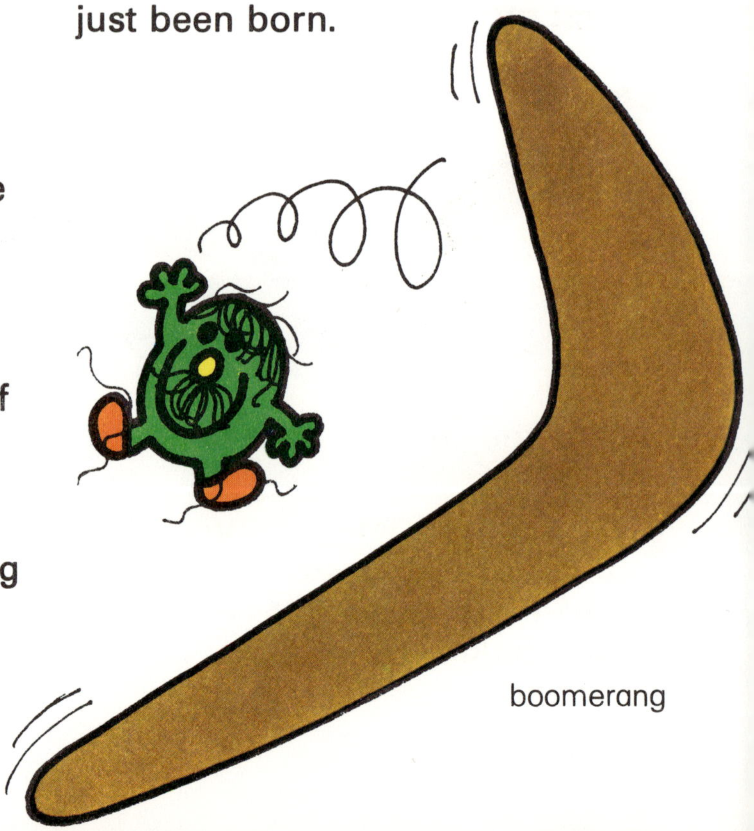
boomerang

Mr Clumsy is throwing a boomerang. "Mind your heads, everybody!"

borrow

To borrow is to take something from someone else to use it, and to give it back afterwards. Mr Happy wanted to borrow Mr Grumpy's lawn mower, but Mr Grumpy wouldn't lend it to him.

bottle

A bottle is used to hold liquid. Bottles are made of glass or plastic. They have a narrow top to make it easy to pour the liquid out.

bottle

bottom

The bottom is the lowest part of something. Mr Clumsy tripped over his shoelaces at the top of the stairs and fell right down to the bottom.

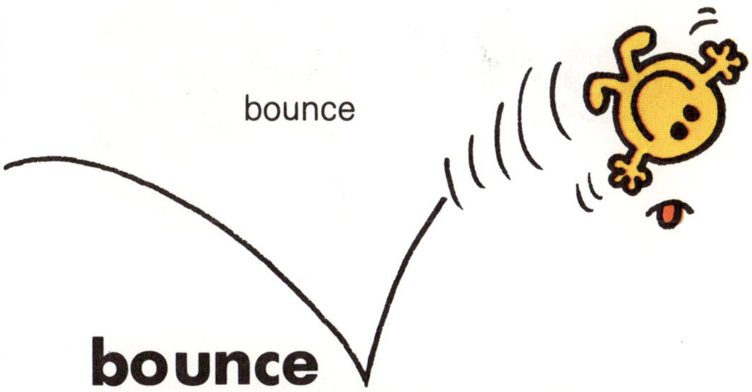

bounce

bounce

To bounce means to jump back into the air after hitting something. Mr Bounce is like a rubber ball. He can't help bouncing wherever he goes.

bow

A bow is a knot with loops. Mr Fussy ties his shoelaces in neat little bows.

A bow is also a piece of bent wood with a string tied from one end to the other. It is used to shoot arrows.

bow

To bow is to bend your body forward at the waist. People bow to the queen.

Bow also means the front end of a boat.

bowl

A bowl is a round dish. Mr Greedy ate a huge bowl of trifle for his tea, and he was still hungry!

box

A box is made of cardboard or wood. A box has four sides, a bottom and top and holds things. Mr Small is so small he can fit inside a box of matches.

box

bracelet

A bracelet is a band or chain worn around the wrist as jewellery. Some bracelets are made of gold or silver.

brain

The brain is part of the body of a person or animal. It is inside the head and controls all the actions of the body. Human beings think, learn and remember with their brains.

brake

A brake is used to slow down the movement of wheels on cars, trains, or bicycles. Most brakes work by pressing a pad against the wheel.

branch

A branch is the part of a tree that grows out from the trunk. Most trees have lots of branches.

Mr Silly is standing on a branch. He is pretending to be a bird!

brave

Brave means not afraid to do something difficult or dangerous. The man jumped into the river to save the boy from drowning. He was very brave.

bread

Bread is a food made by mixing flour and water and then baking it in an oven. You buy a loaf of bread in the shop. You can cut it into slices to make sandwiches or toast.

break

To break something is to make it come apart. Mr Clumsy is always breaking things. His house is full of broken dishes and broken chairs.

breakfast

Breakfast is the first meal of the day. Mr Skinny eats just one cornflake for breakfast. No wonder he is so thin!

This is Mr Skinny's breakfast. One cornflake!

breathe

To breathe is to take in air through your nose or mouth and let it out again. You breathe more quickly when you have been running because you are out of breath.

brick

A brick is a heavy block of hard clay or stone. Bricks are used to build houses. They are usually the same size.

bridge

A bridge is built across a river or a road or a railway. People can then get from one side to the other safely and easily.

bright

Bright means filled with a lot of light. On a fine day the sun shines brightly in the sky.

bring

To bring means to carry something with you when you come. Mr Mean and Mr Forgetful are having a picnic. But Mr Forgetful has forgotten to bring any food and Mr Mean has only brought half a sandwich.

bring

brown

brown

Brown is a colour. It is a mixture of red and green.

bruise

A bruise is a dark mark on the skin, caused by bumping into something. Mr Bump is covered in bruises.

brush

A brush is a tool with stiff hairs at one end and a handle at the other. A brush with a long handle is used to sweep up dirt from the floor. There are many other kinds of brushes, like hairbrushes, toothbrushes and paintbrushes.

bucket

A bucket is a container with a handle. It is often used to carry water. You can use a small bucket to make sand pies at the seaside.

buckle

A buckle is a fastening used to hold together the ends of a belt or a strap. Some shoes fasten with buckles.

budgerigar

A budgerigar is a small brightly coloured bird. It is often kept as a pet. Budgerigars live wild in Australia.

build

To build is to make something by putting smaller parts together. Mr Slow built his house himself. It took him ten years! Slowly . . . brick . . . by . . . brick.

bull

bull

A bull is a male mammal. Bulls are large and have horns. They are kept on farms. Cows belong to the same family as bulls.

bully

A bully is a person who is cruel to others, especially if they are smaller than himself.

bump

To bump into something is to knock into it by accident. Mr Bump had a big bruise on his head after he bumped into a lamp post.

bunch

A bunch is a group of things held together. Mr Quiet is holding a bunch of flowers.

bunch

bundle

A bundle is a group of things that are tied together or wrapped together. Mr Fussy takes a bundle of washing to the laundry each week.

burglar

A burglar is a person who breaks into other people's houses and steals things.

burn

To burn something is to make it so hot that it catches fire. Logs burn when you put them on a fire.

To burn also means to spoil something by letting it get too hot. Mr Forgetful burnt his cakes because he forgot to take them out of the oven.

burst

To burst is to break open. Balloons burst if you put too much air into them or if you prick them with a pin.

bus

bus

A bus is a motor vehicle that takes people from place to place. Buses have lots of seats and people pay money to ride on them.

bush

A bush is a small tree. Its branches start to grow close to the ground. Mr Tickle is hiding behind a bush. He is waiting for someone to tickle.

business

A person's own business is the private things that matter to him only. Mr Nosey is always poking his nose into other people's business. He must learn to mind his own business.

Business is also the work people do to make a living.

bustle

To bustle is to move around in a busy way. Mr Fussy bustled around making everything tidy after Mr Clumsy had gone.

busy

Busy means doing lots of things all the time. Mr Busy has no time to sit and daydream. He is too busy cleaning the house and mowing the lawn and washing the dishes.

butcher

A butcher is a man who sells meat. Mr Noisy has bought some sausages from the butcher's shop.

butter

Butter is a fat made from cream. You can spread butter on bread or buns.

butterfly

butterfly

A butterfly is an insect with a thin body and four large wings. Most butterflies have bright colours on their wings. They fly in the daytime.

button

A button is a small round object. Buttons are sewn on clothes to fasten them.

A button is also a flat knob that you press to make something work. If you press the button on the door, a bell rings.

buy

To buy is to get something by giving money for it. Mr Greedy went to the baker's shop to buy something for his tea. He bought three cream cakes.

butcher

cabbage

cabbage

A cabbage is a vegetable. The leaves of a cabbage make a round head. They are usually green or white. You can eat cabbage either cooked or raw.

cabin

A cabin is a small room on a ship or aeroplane.

cafe

You can buy a snack or a drink in a cafe and eat it or drink it there. Most towns have cafes.

cage

A cage is a metal or wooden enclosure for keeping animals in. The sides of some cages have metal bars.

cake

A cake is a sweet food made from flour and eggs and baked in an oven. Some cakes are flavoured with chocolate or covered with icing. Fruit cakes have raisins and currants in them.

calamity

A calamity is when something very bad happens. When Mr Jelly hears the slightest noise, he thinks it is a calamity. When a leaf brushed past his window, he thought it was an earthquake.

calf

A young cow is called a calf.

Calf also means the back part of your leg, below the knee.

calf

call

When you call out, you say something loudly so that someone far away can hear. Mr Dizzy called for help when a bull chased him out of the field.

To call also means to give someone a name. The Mr Men are all called different names.

To call on is to visit someone. Mr Tall called on Mr Small to see if he would like to go for a walk.

camel

A camel is a large mammal that has one or two humps on its back. In Africa and Asia people ride on camels. They use them to carry heavy loads, especially in the desert.

camera

A camera is used for taking photographs. It looks like a box and it has a special lens at the front. You put a film inside where it is dark.

Mr Clever is taking a picture of Mr Mischief with his camera.

camp

When you camp, you sleep in a tent and live in the open air. Brownies and cub scouts often go to camp in the summer.

canal

A canal is a river made by men. Boats can travel along a canal.

canary

A canary is a small yellow bird. Canaries are sometimes kept as pets in cages.

candle

A candle is a long, thin stick of wax used as a light. It has a string, called the wick, running through the middle of it. The wick burns and gives light.

canoe

A canoe is a light, narrow boat. You move it through the water with a paddle.

capital

A capital is a large letter. A B C are capital letters, a b c are small letters. You use a capital letter at the beginning of a sentence or for a proper name.

The capital of a country is the most important town in that country. Shivertown is the capital of Coldland where Mr Sneeze lives.

capsize

To capsize is to turn over accidentally. Boats capsize. When Mr Happy went to the seaside, he saw a boat capsize. The people in it fell into the water and had to be rescued.

capsize

captain

A captain is the person in charge of a ship or an aeroplane.

The captain of a team is the leader of the team.

capture

To capture a person or animal is to catch him and hold him prisoner.

car

A car is a vehicle driven by an engine. A car has four wheels, doors and seats for the driver and passengers to sit in.

car

caravan

A caravan is a house on wheels. Most caravans can be pulled along by a car. There is room to cook and eat and sleep inside. Some people like to spend their holidays in a caravan. Others live in a caravan all the time.

card

card

A card is a piece of stiff paper. There are many different kinds of cards for all sorts of occasions. You send cards to your friends to wish them Happy Birthday and at Christmas.

When you go on holiday, you send postcards to your friends showing pictures of the places you have visited.

Playing cards are used for card games.

cardboard

Cardboard is very stiff paper. It is used to make boxes.

careful

Careful means thinking about what you are doing. If Mr Clumsy were more careful, he would not break so many things.

careless

Careless means not thinking about what you are doing. Jack got a sum wrong in class. He added 3 and 3 and made it 7. That was a careless mistake.

carol

Carols are the songs that we sing at Christmas.

carpet

A carpet is a covering for the floor. Carpets are usually made of wool or nylon. Some carpets have a pattern on them.

carrot

carrot

A carrot is a vegetable that grows in the ground. The part you eat is the root. Carrots are long and thin and are orange in colour. You can eat carrots raw or cooked.

carry

When you carry something, you hold it while you take it from one place to another. Mr Strong carried Mr Muddle's suitcase for him because it was very heavy.

carry

cartoon

A cartoon is a story or a film made from drawings. Most cartoons are meant to make you laugh. Mr Silly likes watching cartoons on television.

case

A case is a box with a handle. You carry things or store things in a case. When you go on holiday, you take clothes with you in a suitcase.

castle

castle

A castle is a large building with strong, high walls. Castles were built many years ago for kings and queens and rich people. Most castles had a moat all round them to stop enemy soldiers attacking the castle.

cat

Cats are small mammals. They are kept by many people as pets. They have thick fur and sharp claws, and like to catch mice.

catch

To catch is to get hold of something that is moving. Mr Clever can catch a ball with one hand. Isn't he clever!

caterpillar

A caterpillar is the larva of an insect. Most caterpillars have a long, soft body and many pairs of legs. When they are fully grown they turn into butterflies or moths.

cathedral

A cathedral is a large important church. A bishop looks after a cathedral.

cauliflower

A cauliflower is a vegetable. Cauliflowers have a round, white head made up of tiny flowers. This is the part that you eat.

cautious

Cautious means very careful. The children were very cautious before crossing the busy road. They made sure there was no traffic coming before walking across.

cave

A cave is a large hole in rock, big enough to walk in. At the seaside, there are sometimes caves at the bottom of the cliffs. There are also caves in hills and mountains.

ceiling

The ceiling is the inside covering on the top of a room. Mr Impossible can walk on the ceiling. That's impossible!

celebrate

To celebrate is to have a treat because something special has happened. When Mr Small got a new job he had a party to celebrate.

centre

The centre of something is the middle. There is a hole in the centre of a gramophone record.

cereal

A cereal is a plant. It has fruit called grains which we eat. Wheat and corn are cereals. Breakfast cereals, like cornflakes, are made from these grains.

certain

If you are certain of something, you are absolutely sure. If anyone gives Mr Forgetful a message he is certain to forget it.

chain

A chain is a string of metal rings joined together. Chains are used to pull along heavy objects. A chain is also used to connect the pedals of a bicycle with the back wheel, so that when you pedal the bicycle moves along.

chair

chair

A chair is a seat for one person. Chairs have four legs, a seat and a back. Mr Small's chair is about as big as a matchstick.

chance

The chance to do something is the time when it is possible for you to do it. Mr Nosey took the chance to look through the letterbox while there was no one about.

change

To change is to become different. A caterpillar changes into a butterfly when it is fully grown.

To change also means to put on different clothes. When you play football, you change into shorts and a football shirt.

Change is money that you get back when you pay too much. If you give a pound note for a 75p book, you will get 25p change.

charge

To charge is to ask for money when something is being bought. When you want to buy something, you can ask how much the shopkeeper is charging for it.

To charge also means to rush at. When Mr Dizzy went for a walk, a bull lowered its head and charged at him. Mr Dizzy quickly climbed over the gate to safety!

chase

To chase is to run after and try to catch. One day, Mr Mischief took Mr Grumpy's hat and ran away with it. Mr Grumpy had to chase him all the way down the road to get it back.

chat

To chat is to talk in a friendly way. Mr Rush never has time to stop and chat to anyone.

chatter

To chatter is to talk a lot. Mr Chatterbox chatters to everyone, even himself!

cheap

Cheap means not costing very much. Mr Mean always buys the cheapest things he can find.

cheat

To cheat is to do something unfairly. Some people cheat at games.

"Look out, Mr Dizzy! That bull is going to charge at you!"

Mr Fussy is very careful to check his grocery bill before he pays it.

check

When you check something, you make sure that it is right. Mr Fussy checked his grocery bill three times before he paid the shop assistant.

cheek

Your cheek is the part of your face between your nose and your ear. When you blow you puff out your cheeks.

cheerful

Cheerful means happy. Mr Happy is always cheerful but Mr Grumpy can never find anything to be cheerful about.

cheese

Cheese is a food made from milk. There are many different cheeses. Cheddar and Edam are two types you can buy.

chemist

A chemist is a person who makes up medicines. In a chemist's shop you can also buy bandages, soap, toothpaste, films for a camera and lots of other things.

chest

Your chest is the front part of your body between your neck and your waist. Your lungs and your heart are inside your chest. It moves in and out when you breathe.

A chest is also a large strong box. Long ago, pirates hunted for treasure hidden in chests.

The pirates opened the treasure chest and found lots of gold things inside.

chew

To chew is to break up food in your mouth. It takes Mr Slow all evening to eat a currant cake, because he chews each crumb and each currant a hundred times.

chicken

chip

chicken

Chickens are birds that are kept on a farm or in a garden. They lay eggs and their meat can be cooked and eaten.

chief

A chief is a leader, a very important person. Red Indian tribes have chiefs. There are chief policemen and firemen, too.

child

A child is a young boy or girl. When Mr Snow helped Father Christmas, he made sure that all the children got their Christmas presents.

chimney

A chimney is the part of a house built to let the smoke out from a fire. The smoke goes up the chimney from the fireplace and out at the top through a chimney pot.

chin

Your chin is the lowest part of your face, below your mouth and above your neck. Some men grow beards on their chin.

chip

A chip is a small stick of potato fried in hot fat. Mr Greedy finds it hard to walk past a fish and chip shop without going inside and buying some chips.

To chip is to break off small pieces. Most of Mr Clumsy's cups are chipped because he keeps dropping them. Those that aren't chipped are broken!

chocolate

Chocolate is a hard brown sweet made from the seeds of the cocoa plant.

Chocolate is also a drink.

choice

Choice is choosing between two or more things. If you want to buy two toys but only have enough money for one, you have to make a choice between them.

choir

A choir is a group of people who sing together. Boys and girls sometimes sing in a church choir.

choke

To choke is not to be able to breathe properly. When you swallow food the wrong way it makes you choke.

choose

To choose is to pick something you want out of a group. Mr Skinny chose the smallest cake on the plate when he went to tea with Mr Tall.

chop

To chop is to cut something with a quick blow. An axe is used to chop down trees.

To chop also means to cut into small pieces.

A chop is a piece of meat that has a piece of bone in it. You can buy pork chops and lamb chops at the butcher's.

Christmas

Christmas Day is on December 25th. It is the time when Christians remember the birth of Jesus Christ. At Christmas we give our friends presents and send them cards.

chuckle

To chuckle is to laugh quietly to yourself. Mr Mischief chuckled when he thought about all the naughty things he had done.

church

A church is a building where Christians gather on Sundays and other days to sing hymns and pray and hear about God.

cinema

A cinema is a theatre where films are shown on a huge screen.

circle

A circle is a perfect round shape. A ring is a circle.

circus

A circus is a travelling show that takes place inside a big tent. At a circus you can see clowns, acrobats and animals that do tricks.

circus

city

A city is a large town. London and Edinburgh are cities. In Britain any town with a cathedral is called a city.

claim

When you claim something, you say that it belongs to you or that it ought to belong to you.

clap

To clap is to hit the palms of your hands together so that they make a loud noise. People clap to show that they are pleased.

class

A class is any group of people or things that are alike. A class can be a group of children who are taught together at school.

claw

A claw is the sharp, hard point on the foot of an animal or bird. Cats use their claws to scratch with.

clay

Clay is a kind of soft earth. It is used to make bricks. When it is wet it can be used for making models or shaped into useful things like bowls and plates. It becomes very hard if it is baked.

clean

Clean means not dirty. Mr Tidy made Mr Messy have a bath, and he came out looking cleaner than he ever had done before.

clear

Something that is clear can be seen through. Most windows have clear glass in them so that you can see outside.

To clear means to get rid of everything that is in the way. The policeman cleared all the traffic from the road to let the fire engine through.

clearing

A clearing is a part of a wood where there are no trees.

clever

A clever person knows a lot and can do difficult things. Mr Clever thought he knew everything, but he couldn't tell Mr Sneeze how to cure his cold.

cliff

A cliff is a high wall of rock, usually close to the sea. People like to go for a walk along the top of the cliffs.

climb
To climb is to go up something. Mr Daydream climbed up on to the bird's back at the beginning of his adventure.

cling
To cling to means to grip very tightly. Mr Bounce clung to the edge of his chair to stop himself bouncing up to the ceiling.

clip
A clip is a small metal object used to hold things together. A paper clip fastens papers together. A hair clip holds a girl's hair in place.

To clip is to cut something shorter. You clip your nails when they grow too long.

clock
A clock is used to tell the time. It has a face with the numbers 1 to 12 around it, and two hands. The small hand shows you what hour it is, and the big hand points to the minutes past the hour.

clock

close
Close means near to. Mr Nonsense's house is close to Mr Silly's. They do not live very far from each other.

close
To close means to shut. Mr Sneeze closed the door of his house to keep out the cold.

clothes
Clothes are things that you wear. Trousers and dresses and shirts and jeans are clothes. In the winter you wear thick clothes to keep you warm.

cloud
A cloud is a lot of tiny drops of water that float in the sky. Clouds are grey or white. Rain and snow fall from clouds.

clown
A clown is a person who dresses up and does silly tricks to make people laugh. When Mr Funny goes to the circus he likes to watch the clowns best.

club
A club is a group of people who meet to do something together. People who like riding horses can join a riding club.

A club is also a heavy stick. Golf clubs have a rounded head at one end. You hit a small ball with a golf club.

clue

A clue is a hint that helps you to find the answer to a puzzle.

clumsy

Clumsy means awkward or careless. A clumsy person is always knocking things over and bumping into things and breaking things.

coach

A coach is a bus that travels a long way between stops.

To coach people means to help them to be better at something. Football clubs have a coach to help the footballers play a better game.

coal

Coal is a black mineral that is dug from under the ground by miners. When it burns, it makes a bright, warm fire.

coat

You wear a coat over your other clothes to keep you warm.

cocoa

Cocoa is a brown powder made from the seeds of a tree called the cacao or cocoa plant. It is used to make chocolate. You can also mix it with milk and sugar to make a drink.

coconut

A coconut is the fruit of a kind of palm tree. Coconuts are big. They have shells that look like wood. Inside there is white flesh, which you can eat, and a white liquid, called the milk, which you can drink.

code

A code is a set of symbols or words that stand for other words. Codes are used by spies for sending secret messages.

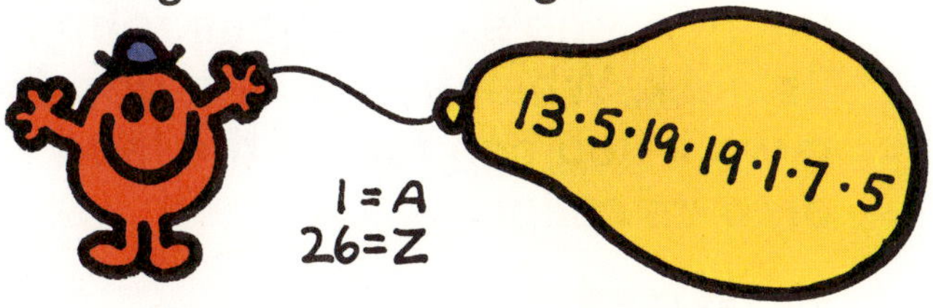

There is a word in code on Mr Small's balloon. Can you work it out?

coffee

Coffee is a drink made with hot water from the beans of a small bush called a coffee tree. It is dark brown and has a strong taste. People often drink coffee with milk or cream.

coin

A coin is a piece of money made of metal such as bronze or silver. Most coins are round, but a 50p piece has seven sides.

collapse

To collapse means to fall down. Mr Rush built a garden shed. In a hurry as usual. When the wind blew, the shed collapsed!

collapse

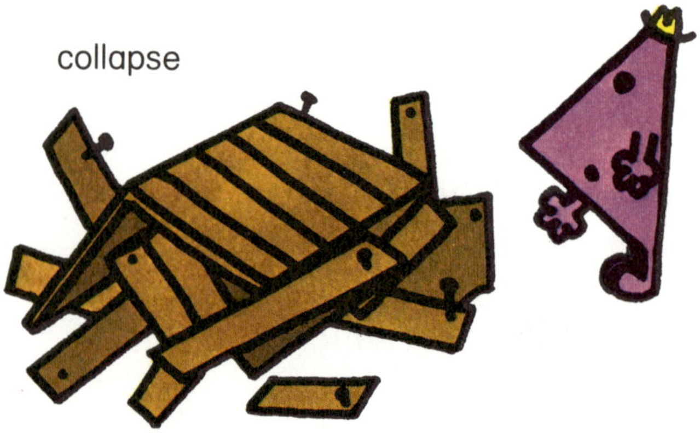

collar

A collar is something that goes round the neck of a person or animal. Shirts have collars on them. A dog's collar goes round its neck. When you take a dog for a walk you can fasten the lead onto its collar.

collect

To collect means to gather together. Some people collect stamps as a hobby and stick them in an album.

collide

To collide means to bump into something. Mr Bump is always colliding with things.

colossal

Colossal means very very big. Mr Greedy has a colossal appetite. He eats more for one meal than an ordinary person would eat all day!

colour

Red and yellow and blue are colours. Green is the colour of grass and white is the colour of snow.

To colour a picture is to put colours on it with crayons or paints. You need red and green crayons to colour a picture of Mr Muddle.

colour

comb

A comb is used to make hair neat and tidy. It has a row of teeth along one edge.

comfortable

To be comfortable is to be at ease. A comfortable chair is soft and pleasant to sit in. You cannot be really comfortable when you are cold or unhappy or in pain.

common

Common means ordinary or found everywhere. A dog is a common pet, but it is not common for people to keep crocodiles in their houses.

Having common sense means being sensible but not too clever. Mr Clever thinks he is very clever. But he doesn't have much common sense. For instance, he doesn't have enough common sense to find his own way home.

commotion

A commotion is a noisy disturbance. Mr Bump caused quite a commotion in the china shop when he knocked over a pile of plates. People in the shop came running to see what was the matter.

company

Company means other people. Mr Busy wanted company on his walk, so he invited Mr Slow to go with him. He did not want to walk alone.

A company is a group of people who work together.

competition

A competition is a test to find out who is best or first. The winner is often given a prize.

complain

To complain is to grumble because you don't like something. Mr Fussy complained that his marmalade had untidy bits of peel in it. He made a complaint to the shop.

complete

To complete means to finish. Mr Rush never completes anything properly. He just rushes from one job to the next.

Complete means having everything there. The jigsaw puzzle was complete. No pieces were missing.

Completely means totally. The cake was completely covered in chocolate.

compliment

A compliment is something good said to praise someone. If a person does good work, he likes to be complimented on it.

Mr Silly entered the 'Silliest Idea of the Year' competition and he won the Nonsense Cup.

computer

A computer is a machine that is used to solve many problems and provide information at high speed.

Mr Clever showed Mr Funny his clever new computer. He said it could even tell Mr Funny some new jokes!

concentrate

To concentrate means to pay attention. Your teacher likes you to concentrate in class all the time.

concern

To concern means to have something to do with. Mr Nosey is always prying into things that do not concern him.

Concerned means worried. Mr Worry was concerned about Mr Noisy. He was afraid Mr Noisy might lose his voice because he shouted so loudly.

condition

The condition of something is the way it is. Mr Messy's house is not in very good condition. There are tiles missing from the roof and the windows are broken.

confess

To confess is to own up that you have done something wrong. The wizard made Mr Mischief confess that it was he who filled Mr Funny's hat with treacle.

cook

To cook is to make food ready to eat by heating it in the oven or in a pan on the stove. In Sleepyland it takes three hours to cook a boiled egg and a whole day to cook roast chicken!

co-operate

To co-operate means to work with someone else in a helpful way. It is much easier to work as a team if everyone co-operates.

cope

To cope means to manage. Mr Busy can cope with lots of jobs around the house. He can make his bed, clean the windows and bake a cake. All before breakfast!

copy

To copy is to make something look the same as something else. Can you copy some of the pictures of the Mr Men in this book?

A copy of something is exactly the same as the original. You can have copies of a photograph printed, so that you can give them to friends.

copy

corner

A corner is the
sides or walls m
four corners.

cornflake

Cornflakes are
eaten with milk
breakfast time.
from grains of
America is calle

correct

Correct means
not very clever.
asks him a ques
knows the corre

To correct so
put them right.
like to be able t
all the time. But
doesn't know th

corridor

A corridor is a
inside a buildin
usually have ro

cost

The cost of som
amount of mon
it. That is what
bought all the f
house. It cost hi

costume

A costume is a
dress. When you
fancy-dress part
the costume of
cowboy or a clo

confident

Confident means being sure that you can do something. Mr Rush was confident that he could run faster than Mr Slow. He was right to be confident. He beat Mr Slow by six hours!

confuse

To confuse is to make someone muddled. Mr Silly was rather confused when he came to a silly signpost in Nonsenseland. All the roads led to nowhere! He didn't know which way to go. How confusing!

confuse

congratulations

Congratulations are good wishes given to someone who has done something like passing a test or winning a competition or getting married.

conjuror

A conjuror is a person who does magic tricks. Everyone clapped when the conjuror pulled a rabbit out of his hat.

consider

To consider something is to think about it carefully. Before buying a sausage for his dinner, Mr Mean considered whether he could afford it or not.

considerable

Considerable means quite large. Mr Uppity has a considerable amount of money in the bank.

consist

To consist of means to be made up of. A sewing kit consists of things like needles, pins and cottons.

contain

To contain means to hold or to have inside. Mr Skinny's food cupboard contains only half a packet of biscuits and a few crumbs of bread. That should last him for a week!

contented

Contented means pleased and happy. Mr Greedy was contented after his enormous meal.

conjuror

contents

The contents of something are the things that are inside it. Mr Nonsense emptied out the contents of his piggy bank and found he had two buttons, a safety pin and three matchsticks in there.

contest

A contest is a game or a race that somebody tries to win. Mr Strong and Mr Happy had a contest to see who could lift the heaviest weight. Mr Strong won. He lifted a huge bag of coal with his little finger!

contest

continue

To continue is to carry on doing something. Mr Chatterbox continued to talk even after everyone had gone away.

contradict

To contradict someone is to say that he is wrong.

Mr Topsy Tur
aeroplane. He
over the place

control

To control s
charge of it
control his
starts to fly

Controls
for guiding

conven

Convenient
handy. A h
convenient
use as a sh

conver

A conversat
people.

convin

To convince
something i
it. Mr Wron
a flowerpot
Right convir
was a flowe

cottage

A cottage is a small house. You often find cottages in country villages.

cotton

Cotton is a cloth made from the fluffy seeds of a plant. Cotton thread is used for sewing.

Cotton wool is the fluffy white part of the cotton plant after it has been cleaned but before it is made into thread or cloth.

count

To count is to find out how many there are. Mr Mean spends hours counting the gold coins in his box. He likes to know how much money he has but he doesn't like to spend it.

count

counter

A counter is a long table in a shop. The shop assistant usually stands behind the counter to serve customers.

A counter is also a small round plastic object. Counters are used in games like tiddlywinks.

country

country

A country is an area of land that has its own government. England and France and Spain are all different countries.

The country also means land outside towns and cities. There are fields and hills and farms in the country.

couple

A couple means two things or people that go together. A married couple is a husband and wife.

court

A court is an area of ground surrounded by walls or buildings.

A tennis court is a rectangular piece of ground where tennis is played. There is a net across the middle of the court and white lines are marked on the ground.

cover

To cover something is to put something else over it to keep it clean or dry or warm.

cupboard

A cupboard is a closed piece of furniture with shelves inside. It is used to store things like food and cups and plates. Everything is arranged very neatly inside Mr Fussy's cupboard.

cupboard

cure

To cure a sick person or animal means to make him well again.

curious

Curious means wanting to know about something. Mr Nosey was curious about his new neighbours. So he peeped through their letterbox to see if he could see them.

Curious also means strange or unusual. Mr Happy heard a curious squeaking noise outside. But it was only the branch of a tree blowing in the wind.

This pig has a curly tail.

curl

To curl is to twist into a curved shape. Lots of women curl their hair because they don't like it straight. Other people have naturally curly hair.

currant

Currants are small grapes that have been dried in the sun. They are used in some cakes and buns.

curse

To put a curse on someone is to wish that something bad will happen to him.

curtain

A curtain is made from material and hung at a window. You draw the curtains back to let in the light.

cushion

A cushion is a soft pad put on a chair to make it more comfortable or higher.

custard

Custard is a sweet yellow sauce made with milk. You can pour custard over pies and puddings.

customer

A customer is a person who buys something. There is a long queue of customers in the baker's shop.

crow
A crow is a large black bird. It makes a loud, sharp cry.

crowd
A crowd is a large group of people. There were crowds of people enjoying themselves at the fair.

Crowded means full of people. It is hot and stuffy on a crowded bus.

crown
A crown is worn on the head by a king or queen. Crowns are usually made of gold and precious jewels.

crown

cruel
Cruel means very unkind. It is cruel to pull a dog's tail. It is painful for the dog.

crumb
A crumb is a very small piece of bread or cake. Mr Messy always drops crumbs on the table when he eats a biscuit.

crunch
To crunch something is to chew it noisily. You make a crunching noise when you eat crisps.

crush
To crush is to squeeze something tightly. Your clothes will be creased after being crushed into a suitcase.

crust
The crust is the crisp outside part of a loaf of bread. Mr Fussy always cuts the crusts off his sandwiches.

cry
When you cry, tears come out of your eyes because you are unhappy or in pain. The little girl cried when she fell off her swing.

To cry also means to shout. Mr Happy cried, "Careful Mr Bump!" when he saw him climbing a tree.

cuckoo
A cuckoo is a bird. It lays its eggs in other birds' nests. When the cuckoo calls it says "cuckoo".

cucumber
Cucumbers are long green salad vegetables. You can grow them in the garden or in a greenhouse.

cunning
Cunning means being clever at fooling other people. Mr Mischief is very cunning. He is always playing tricks on people, but nobody ever catches him.

creep

To creep is to move slowly and quietly. Mr Mischief crept round the side of Mr Jelly's house and hid in the bushes. He wanted to surprise Mr Jelly when he came out.

crest

The crest is the top of something. Some birds have a crest of skin or feathers on their heads.

crest

crew

A crew is a team of people who work together. The crew of a boat or an aeroplane are the people who make it go and look after the passengers.

criminal

A criminal is a person who has done something wrong and been sent to prison.

crisp

Crisp means hard but easily broken. Biscuits are crisp when they are fresh.

Crisps are very thin pieces of potato that have been fried in hot fat. You can buy bags of crisps in many different flavours.

criticise

To criticise something is to say why you don't like it – or why you do.

crocodile

A crocodile is a large reptile that lives in water or on the land near to water. It has strong jaws with lots of sharp teeth.

crocodile

cross

To cross is to go from one side of something to another. Look carefully before you cross the road!

A cross is a mark like an X.

Cross also means rather angry. Mr Grumpy is always cross about something, he is so bad-tempered.

crossroads

A crossroads is the place where two roads going in different directions pass over each other.

crossroads

cow

cow

A cow is a female mammal. Cows eat grass and produce milk for us to drink. They are kept on farms and have to be milked every day.

coward

A coward is a person who is not very brave. Sometimes cowards want to do something difficult or dangerous but they are too frightened.

cowboy

A cowboy is a man who looks after cattle on a ranch in America.

crack

To crack is to break something a little bit but not into pieces. When Mr Clumsy dropped a basket of eggs he cracked three and broke six.

A crack is a small, narrow opening in something or the space between two things that are close together. Mr Nosey peeped between the crack in the fence to see what was going on.

cramp

Cramp is a sharp pain in a muscle. You sometimes get cramp in your legs when you go swimming.

crash

A crash is when two or more things collide with each other suddenly. The sound of things crashing sometimes makes a very loud noise. When Mr Strong kicked a ball, it crashed through the window.

crawl

To crawl is to move along on your hands and knees. Most babies crawl before they learn to walk.

crawl

crazy

Crazy means completely mad. Mr Nonsense does crazy things like using his bed as a toboggan.

cream

Cream is the thick, tasty part of milk with fat in it. It comes to the top of milk when it is left standing. Butter and cheese are made from cream.

creature

A creature is any kind of animal. Fish are creatures that live in the sea.

crow

A crow is a large black bird. It makes a loud, sharp cry.

crowd

A crowd is a large group of people. There were crowds of people enjoying themselves at the fair.

Crowded means full of people. It is hot and stuffy on a crowded bus.

crown

A crown is worn on the head by a king or queen. Crowns are usually made of gold and precious jewels.

crown

cruel

Cruel means very unkind. It is cruel to pull a dog's tail. It is painful for the dog.

crumb

A crumb is a very small piece of bread or cake. Mr Messy always drops crumbs on the table when he eats a biscuit.

crunch

To crunch something is to chew it noisily. You make a crunching noise when you eat crisps.

crush

To crush is to squeeze something tightly. Your clothes will be creased after being crushed into a suitcase.

crust

The crust is the crisp outside part of a loaf of bread. Mr Fussy always cuts the crusts off his sandwiches.

cry

When you cry, tears come out of your eyes because you are unhappy or in pain. The little girl cried when she fell off her swing.

To cry also means to shout. Mr Happy cried, "Careful Mr Bump!" when he saw him climbing a tree.

cuckoo

A cuckoo is a bird. It lays its eggs in other birds' nests. When the cuckoo calls it says "cuckoo".

cucumber

Cucumbers are long green salad vegetables. You can grow them in the garden or in a greenhouse.

cunning

Cunning means being clever at fooling other people. Mr Mischief is very cunning. He is always playing tricks on people, but nobody ever catches him.

cupboard

A cupboard is a closed piece of furniture with shelves inside. It is used to store things like food and cups and plates. Everything is arranged very neatly inside Mr Fussy's cupboard.

cupboard

cure

To cure a sick person or animal means to make him well again.

curious

Curious means wanting to know about something. Mr Nosey was curious about his new neighbours. So he peeped through their letterbox to see if he could see them.

Curious also means strange or unusual. Mr Happy heard a curious squeaking noise outside. But it was only the branch of a tree blowing in the wind.

This pig has a curly tail.

curl

To curl is to twist into a curved shape. Lots of women curl their hair because they don't like it straight. Other people have naturally curly hair.

currant

Currants are small grapes that have been dried in the sun. They are used in some cakes and buns.

curse

To put a curse on someone is to wish that something bad will happen to him.

curtain

A curtain is made from material and hung at a window. You draw the curtains back to let in the light.

cushion

A cushion is a soft pad put on a chair to make it more comfortable or higher.

custard

Custard is a sweet yellow sauce made with milk. You can pour custard over pies and puddings.

customer

A customer is a person who buys something. There is a long queue of customers in the baker's shop.

cow

cow

A cow is a female mammal. Cows eat grass and produce milk for us to drink. They are kept on farms and have to be milked every day.

coward

A coward is a person who is not very brave. Sometimes cowards want to do something difficult or dangerous but they are too frightened.

cowboy

A cowboy is a man who looks after cattle on a ranch in America.

crack

To crack is to break something a little bit but not into pieces. When Mr Clumsy dropped a basket of eggs he cracked three and broke six.

A crack is a small, narrow opening in something or the space between two things that are close together. Mr Nosey peeped between the crack in the fence to see what was going on.

cramp

Cramp is a sharp pain in a muscle. You sometimes get cramp in your legs when you go swimming.

crash

A crash is when two or more things collide with each other suddenly. The sound of things crashing sometimes makes a very loud noise. When Mr Strong kicked a ball, it crashed through the window.

crawl

To crawl is to move along on your hands and knees. Most babies crawl before they learn to walk.

crawl

crazy

Crazy means completely mad. Mr Nonsense does crazy things like using his bed as a toboggan.

cream

Cream is the thick, tasty part of milk with fat in it. It comes to the top of milk when it is left standing. Butter and cheese are made from cream.

creature

A creature is any kind of animal. Fish are creatures that live in the sea.

creep

To creep is to move slowly and quietly. Mr Mischief crept round the side of Mr Jelly's house and hid in the bushes. He wanted to surprise Mr Jelly when he came out.

crest

The crest is the top of something. Some birds have a crest of skin or feathers on their heads.

crest

crew

A crew is a team of people who work together. The crew of a boat or an aeroplane are the people who make it go and look after the passengers.

criminal

A criminal is a person who has done something wrong and been sent to prison.

crisp

Crisp means hard but easily broken. Biscuits are crisp when they are fresh.

Crisps are very thin pieces of potato that have been fried in hot fat. You can buy bags of crisps in many different flavours.

criticise

To criticise something is to say why you don't like it – or why you do.

crocodile

A crocodile is a large reptile that lives in water or on the land near to water. It has strong jaws with lots of sharp teeth.

crocodile

cross

To cross is to go from one side of something to another. Look carefully before you cross the road!

A cross is a mark like an X.

Cross also means rather angry. Mr Grumpy is always cross about something, he is so bad-tempered.

crossroads

A crossroads is the place where two roads going in different directions pass over each other.

crossroads

daffodil

A daffodil is a yellow spring flower. It grows from a bulb.

daily

Daily means happening every day. Mr Busy cleans his house daily. Every morning he cleans it from top to bottom.

daisy

A daisy is a small flower. It has a yellow centre with lots of white petals around it. Mr Small lives in a house under a daisy. It's a very small house indeed.

daisy

damage

To damage means to break something or stop it working properly. Mr Bump damaged his clock when he dropped it on the floor.

damp

Damp means slightly wet. In the early morning the dew makes the grass damp.

dance

To dance is to move around in time to music. People dance to music at parties.

dandelion

A dandelion is a bright yellow flower. Dandelions grow like weeds in my garden.

dangerous

Something that is dangerous is likely to hurt people. Broken glass is dangerous. You can cut yourself on it.

dare

To dare is to be brave enough to do something. Mr Jelly heard a strange noise outside but he did not dare to go and see what it was. He's not very daring at all.

dark

Dark means having no light. It is very dark at night when there is no moon.

date

The date is a particular day of the month. The date of Christmas Day is December 25th.

Another kind of date is a sweet, sticky fruit. Dates grow at the top of palm trees.

daydream

To daydream is to dream while you are awake. You think you are somewhere else doing something different. Mr Daydream is always daydreaming about adventures, instead of listening to what people are saying to him.

daze

To daze is to make someone dizzy or confused. Mr Bump was dazed after he hit his head on a lamp post. He couldn't remember where he was or what day it was.

dead

Dead means no longer alive. In autumn the dead leaves fall from the trees.

deaf

Deaf means not able to hear. Deaf people can learn to understand others by watching their lips move and by using sign language.

dear

Dear means costing a lot of money.

Dear is also a word you use for someone you are fond of.

death

Death is the end of life. Everyone in the country was upset at the death of the old king.

decide

To decide is to make up your mind. Mr Greedy could not decide whether to have a chocolate cake or a cream cake for his tea. So he ate both!

decorate

To decorate something means to make it look pretty. On his birthday, Mr Chatterbox had a birthday cake decorated with icing and candles.

deep

Deep means going down a long way. Diving into deep water is fun, as long as you are a good swimmer.

definite

Definite means certain. Mr Happy hopes to have a holiday sometime during the summer, but he has not yet made any definite arrangements.

delay

To delay is to make late. Last winter, the school bus was delayed three times because of the ice and snow.

To delay also means to put off to a later time.

deliberately

Deliberately means on purpose. Mr Mischief deliberately bumped into Mr Fussy and made him drop his shopping basket.

delicate

Delicate means beautiful but easily hurt or damaged. Glasses made of very thin glass are delicate.

delicious

Delicious means good to eat or to smell. Mr Greedy sat down to a delicious meal of sausages, peas and chips.

deliver

To deliver is to carry something and give it to someone at his address. Mr Snow helped Father Christmas to deliver the children's Christmas presents.

demand

To demand means to ask for as a right. Mr Uppity found that one of the eggs he had bought had a crack in it, so he demanded his money back from the grocer.

dentist

A dentist is a person who looks after people's teeth. Mr Greedy went to the dentist when he had toothache. The dentist told him he had been eating too many sweets. He put a filling in Mr Greedy's tooth and made it better.

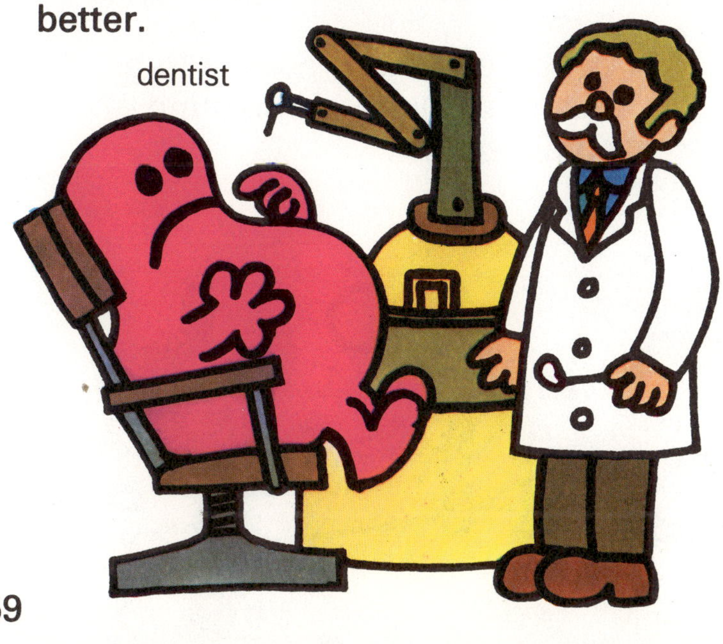

department

A department is just a part of a school or an office or a shop. A really big shop has different departments to sell shoes, clothes, toys, books and other things.

depend

To depend on means to rely on someone or something. Young animals depend on their parents for food. They must have their parents to look after them.

Depend also means to be influenced by. We may be able to have a picnic tomorrow, but it depends on the weather.

describe

To describe something means to say what it is like. Can you describe your friend?

desert

A desert is a hot, dry, sandy land with very few plants growing on it. Very little water is found in the desert.

To desert also means to go away and leave something or somebody.

deserted

Deserted means completely empty. The streets were deserted during the storm. Everyone stayed inside to keep warm and dry.

deserve

To deserve means to have a right to. Mr Lazy felt that he deserved an hour's rest after spending a whole five minutes working in the garden.

design

To design something means to draw or make a plan of how you are going to make it. Aeroplane designers draw designs before they start building a new plane.

desk

A desk is a piece of furniture that you work at. It has a flat top where you can read, write or draw and it usually has drawers for keeping books and pens in.

desk

despair

To despair is to give up hope. Mr Dizzy despairs of ever being clever.

destroy

To destroy means to ruin completely. A fire destroyed a whole row of buildings in the town.

detail

A detail is a very small part of something. The artist has drawn a picture of the sweetshop in detail. He has drawn every single jar of sweets, with all the sweets inside!

detective

detective

A detective is a policeman who looks for information so that crimes can be solved. He looks for clues and questions people.

determined

To be determined is to make up your mind and not to change it. Mr Bounce was determined to find out how he could stop bouncing all the time. So he went to the doctor for help.

detest

To detest something is to hate it very much. I detest lumpy porridge!

dial

A dial is the face of a clock or the front of a telephone. It is marked with numbers.

To dial a number on the telephone you put your finger on the number you want and move the dial right round.

diary

A diary is a book with a space for each day of the year. In a diary you can write down what you have to remember to do each day. You can also write in your diary all the things you have thought about or done.

dictionary

A dictionary is a book that tells you what words mean and how they are used and spelt. This book is a dictionary, the words are in alphabetical order.

die

To die is to stop living. Plants die if they cannot get enough water.

diet

A diet is the food we eat. People who are fat sometimes go on a special diet to help them get thinner.

different
Different means not the same. Mr Silly and Mr Nonsense do the same kind of silly things, but they look very different.

difficult
Difficult means not easy. It is difficult to carry four glasses of water at the same time in your hands.

dig
To dig means to make a hole in the ground. Mr Topsy Turvy is trying to dig a hole in his garden. But his spade is upside down!

dig

dinner
Dinner is the main meal of the day. People often eat meat and vegetables for dinner.

dinosaur
A dinosaur was a very large reptile that lived millions of years ago. There were many different kinds of dinosaurs, and some of them were the biggest animals that ever lived on the earth.

dip
To dip is to put something into a liquid for a moment and take it out again. Mr Silly dipped his finger into his glass of lemonade to make sure it was wet!

direction
The direction of something is the way it is going. Mr Wrong decided to go to the shops but he set off in the wrong direction!

dirty
Dirty means not clean. Mr Messy's house is always dirty because he never does any cleaning.

disagree
To disagree means to think differently about something. Mr Tall and Mr Small disagreed about where to go for their holiday. Mr Tall wanted to go to the country and Mr Small wanted to go to the seaside. So they agreed to have a week at each place.

dinosaur

disappear

To disappear means to go out of sight. Nobody believed Mr Impossible when he said he could make himself invisible. But he proved it by disappearing in front of their very eyes!

disappoint

To disappoint is to make someone upset because what they expected did not actually happen. Mr Greedy was disappointed when he found the baker's shop was closed. He had been looking forward to buying some more cream cakes.

disapprove

To disapprove of something means to think it is wrong or not good. Mr Busy disapproves of Mr Lazy's staying in bed until midday.

disaster

A disaster is something terrible that happens suddenly, like a plane crash or an earthquake.

discover

To discover means to find something for the first time. Mr Muddle discovered that ice cream melts when it gets hot. He put it in the oven instead of the fridge by mistake!

discussion

A discussion is talking things over with other people. The people of Tiddletown had a discussion about Mr Nosey and his prying ways.

disease

A disease is an illness. Measles is a disease that many children have.

disgrace

When you are in disgrace, people are cross with you for doing something bad. Mr Mischief was in disgrace at the party for putting salt into the lemonade.

disguise

To disguise yourself is to change the way you look so that other people won't know who you are. Mr Chatterbox tried to disguise himself by wearing a false moustache. But everyone knew it was Mr Chatterbox in disguise, because he talked so much!

disguise

disgust

Disgust is a feeling of being shocked by something. Bullying smaller children is a disgusting way to behave.

dislike

To dislike means not to like. Mr Lazy dislikes doing anything that means hard work.

disobedient

Disobedient means not doing as you are told. Disobedient children sometimes play with their friends after school, even though their mothers have told them to come straight home.

distance

The distance between two places or things is the amount of space between them.

In the distance means far away. As the train came round the corner the passengers could see the sea in the distance.

disturb

To disturb means to interrupt. Mr Lazy was dropping off to sleep when the sound of the telephone disturbed him.

To disturb also means to upset.

ditch

A ditch is a long, narrow channel dug in the ground. There is a ditch alongside most country roads for rain water to drain into.

dive

To dive is to go into water head first.

dizzy

Dizzy means feeling as if you are going to fall over. You will feel dizzy if you spin round and round very quickly. Mr Dizzy feels dizzy because everyone else seems so clever and makes him feel silly. It makes his head spin.

doctor

A doctor is a person who treats people who are sick or hurt.

dog

A dog is a mammal. Dogs are kept as pets or to guard the house. There are many different kinds of dogs. Some are quite small, like corgis, and some are very big, like alsatians.

doll

A doll is a toy that looks like a little person. Children play with dolls and dress them up in different clothes.

dolphin

A dolphin is an animal that lives in the sea. Dolphins look like fish, but in fact they are mammals. They are very friendly and very intelligent. They like to do tricks and play.

donkey

A donkey is an animal that looks like a small grey horse. Donkeys have long ears and are used in some countries to carry things.

double

Double means twice as big or twice as much. Two people can sleep in a double bed but only one person can sleep in a single bed.

doubtful

Doubtful means not sure about something. Mr Happy thought it was warm enough to go for a swim but Mr Worry was doubtful. He thought the sea would be cold and that everyone might catch a chill.

doughnut

A doughnut is a small round cake. Some doughnuts have a hole in the middle. Doughnuts are fried in fat instead of being baked in an oven. They usually have jam or cream in them.

down

Down means going from a higher part to a lower part. It is fun to slide down a hill on a toboggan.

downright

Downright means absolutely. Mr Uppity is not just unfriendly, he is downright rude.

downstairs

Downstairs means going from the top of the stairs to the bottom. Mr Clumsy is always tripping over his shoelaces and falling downstairs.

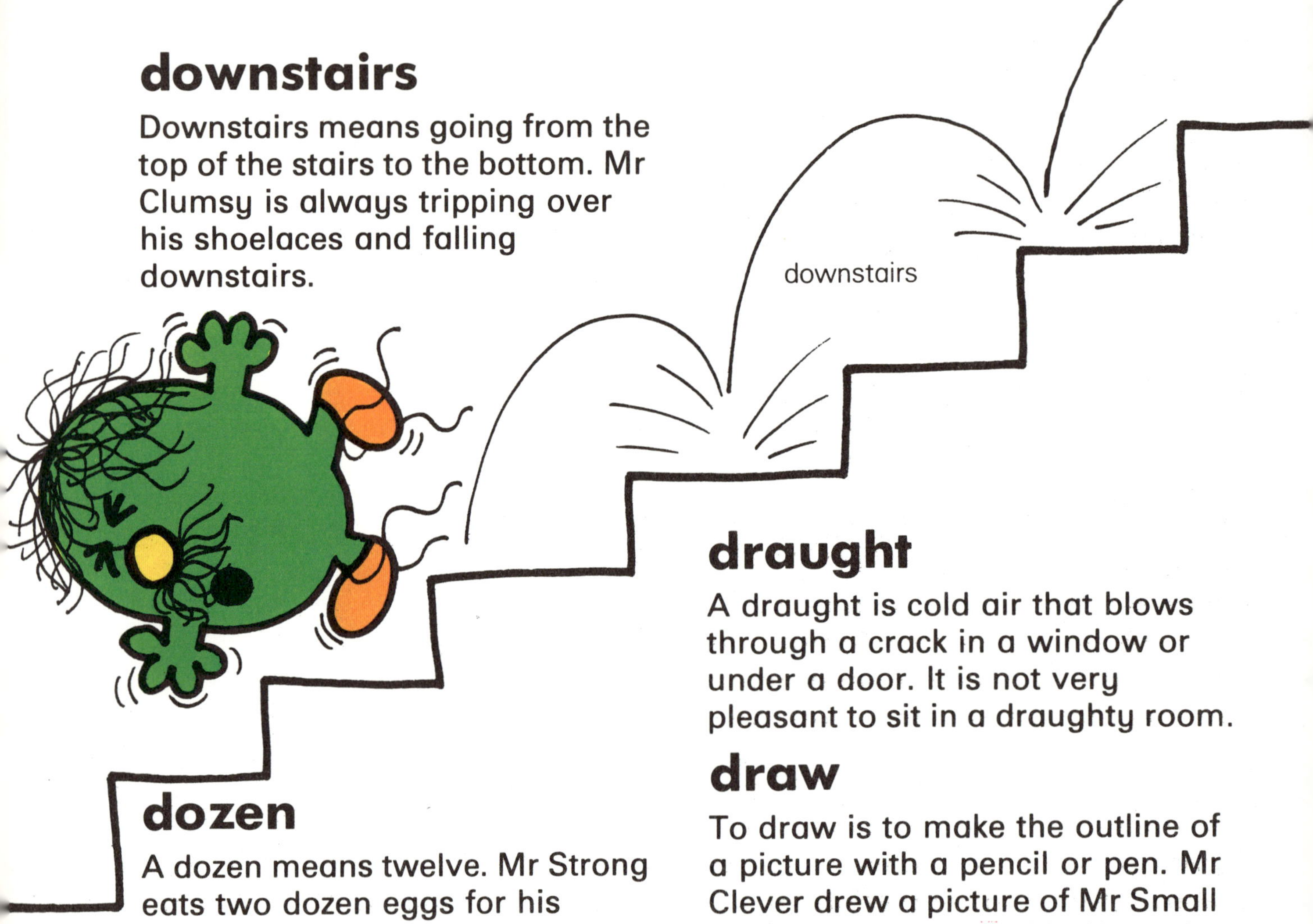

draught

A draught is cold air that blows through a crack in a window or under a door. It is not very pleasant to sit in a draughty room.

dozen

A dozen means twelve. Mr Strong eats two dozen eggs for his breakfast every day.

drag

To drag means to pull heavy things. Mr Slow helped Mr Skinny to drag the table across the room.

dragon

A dragon is an animal that is only found in stories. Dragons have large, scaly bodies and wings and they breathe fire.

draw

To draw is to make the outline of a picture with a pencil or pen. Mr Clever drew a picture of Mr Small to hang on his wall. Mr Clever is good at drawing. He can draw pictures of nearly all the Mr Men.

A drawing is a picture that has been drawn by someone.

drawer

A drawer is a long, flat box without a top. It fits into a piece of furniture. Drawers have handles so they can be pulled out and pushed in.

dreadful

Dreadful means very bad. Mr Grumpy tore all the pages out of his book. It was a dreadful thing to do.

dream

To dream is to think of things while you are asleep. Mr Lazy dreamt that he was made to go on a long walk. He was very pleased when he found it was only a dream.

dream

drive

drive

To drive a car is to use the controls to make it move along. When Mr Bump got his first car he drove straight into a lamp post. He had never driven before!

dress

To dress is to put on clothes. In the winter you have to dress in warm clothes.

A dress is a piece of clothing that women and girls wear. It has a skirt and a top all in one piece.

drink

To drink is to swallow liquid. Mr Rush was very thirsty after all his running around. He drank three glasses of lemonade before rushing off again.

drip

A drip is liquid falling as a very small drop. The noise of the dripping tap kept Mr Quiet awake all night.

droop

To droop is to hang down sadly. After two weeks without rain, the flowers in the garden were drooping.

drop

To drop something is to let it fall. Mr Clumsy dropped a tin of beans on his foot and had a big bruise on his toe for days afterwards.

A drop is a tiny ball of liquid. Rain falls in drops from the sky.

drought

A drought is a long time without rain.

drown

To drown is to die under water because you cannot breathe. Mr Jelly thought he was going to drown when he fell in the duckpond. But it wasn't very deep and he was able to get out quite easily.

drum

A drum is a musical instrument. It makes a low thumping noise when you hit it with a stick. Drums are used for rhythm in music.

dry

Dry means not wet. Mr Tall came home and changed into dry shoes after his walk in the rain.

To dry something means to make it dry. After a swim you dry yourself on a towel.

duck

A duck is a bird that can swim. Ducks have webbed feet so that they can swim on rivers and ponds. Ducks do not live in the water all the time. They make a loud quacking noise.

dull

Dull means not bright or shiny. On a dull day the sky is grey and the sun does not shine.

Dull also means not interesting. The book Mr Quiet was reading was so dull, he fell asleep before he had finished it.

during

During means within a period of time. Many people take their holidays during the summer.

dust

Dust is very tiny bits of dirt. You can sometimes see dust on furniture. There is never a speck of dust to be seen in Mr Fussy's house. He even dusts the flowers in the garden!

each

Each means every one. There is a story about each of the Mr Men.

ear

You have two ears, one on each side of your head. Your ears help you to listen.

early

Early means before the right time. Mr Worry was worried that he would be late for the party. So he arrived two hours early!

Early also means first thing in the morning. Mr Lazy doesn't like getting up early.

earn

To earn something is to get it by working for it. Mr Rush tried to find a job so that he could earn enough money to go on holiday.

earth

We live on a planet called earth. It is a huge round body that moves around the sun.

Earth is also another word for soil. Mr Messy is covered in earth because he has been working in the garden.

earthquake

An earthquake is a movement of the earth's surface that makes the ground shake. If there is a bad earthquake, buildings fall down.

Easter

Easter is the time of the year when Christians remember the death of Jesus Christ and his rising from the dead. Easter is always in the spring, in March or April. At Easter, the shops sell Easter eggs made of chocolate.

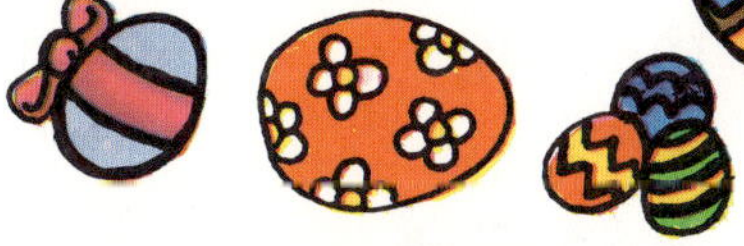

easy

You do not have to work very hard to do something easy. Some words are very easy to read, but others are more difficult.

earth

eat

To eat is to take food into the mouth, chew it and swallow it. We must eat to keep alive. Mr Greedy had eaten three packets of chocolate biscuits. He is always eating!

echo

An echo is the same sound coming back again. If you shout in a cave you will hear an echo of your own voice coming back a few seconds later. Echoes are caused by sound waves bouncing back off a wall or cliff.

edge

The edge of something is the place where it ends. A knife has a sharp edge. If you stand too near the edge of a cliff, you might fall over.

effort

When you make an effort you try very hard to do something. It takes a lot of effort to lift a heavy object.

egg

We eat eggs that have been laid by hens. Other birds lay eggs as well. So do fish and reptiles. If kept warm for a time, eggs hatch into baby birds or animals.

either

Either means one or the other of two. You may either go to the fair or have a picnic, but you cannot do both.

elbow

Your elbow is the middle part of your arm that bends.

electricity

Electricity is a kind of power. Light bulbs, washing machines and televisions need electricity to make them work.

Electric means using electricity. Electric trains run by electricity.

elephant

An elephant is a very large heavy mammal with a long trunk and two tusks. There are two kinds of elephant, one lives in Africa and the other lives in Asia.

elephant

embarrassed

When you are embarrassed you feel silly and uncomfortable about yourself. You may feel that everyone is looking at you. Some people blush when they are embarrassed.

There was an emergency at the farm. Mr Rush raced along to put out the fire.

emergency

An emergency is something serious that happens without warning. You have to move quickly in an emergency. A fire or a road accident is an emergency.

empty

Something that is empty has nothing inside it. Mr Greedy cannot bear to see empty shelves in his food cupboard.

encourage

To encourage means to give someone courage and helpful advice. Mr Happy encouraged Mr Clever to enter for the quiz competition because he thought Mr Clever would win it.

end

The end is the last part of something. At the end of the play, the audience clapped loudly.
To end means to finish. Mr Happy loves books that end happily.

enemy

Your enemy is something or someone that intends to do you harm. A country may go to war to fight its enemy.

engine

An engine is the part of a car or train or aeroplane that makes it move. Engines work by burning oil or petrol or by using electricity.

enjoy

To enjoy something is to like doing it. Mr Tickle enjoys tickling people. But not everyone enjoys being tickled!

enormous

Enormous means very big indeed. Mr Greedy has an enormous appetite but Mr Skinny has hardly any appetite at all.

enough

Enough means as much as is needed. Mr Mean bought only one carrot. He said it would be quite enough for lunch. For six people!

enter

To enter is to go in. Everyone laughed when Mr Topsy Turvy entered the room backwards.

envelope

An envelope is a paper packet. You put a letter in an envelope before you post it. You write the name and address of the person you are sending the letter to on the outside of the envelope.

envy

To envy is to think someone is luckier than you. Everybody envied Peter when he was given a new bicycle for Christmas.

equal

Equal means exactly the same. Mr Silly and Mr Nonsense shared the cake equally between them. They both had exactly the same amount of cake to eat.

equipment

The equipment is all the special items required to do a job or play a game.

error

An error is a mistake. Mr Uppity complained to the manager of the hotel because there was an error in his bill.

escalator

An escalator is a moving staircase. In shops it is used to carry people from one floor to another. This saves them walking up or down lots of stairs.

escape

To escape means to get away. Mr Mischief escaped from Mr Busy. He ran away as fast as his little legs would carry him.

especially

Especially means in particular or more than normally. Mr Rush loves trains, especially express trains because they go so fast!

essential

Essential means most important or necessary. It is essential to brush your teeth every day to keep them clean and healthy.

estate

An estate is an area of land. A housing estate is an area of a town with many houses on it.

even

An even number can be divided by two. Six and ten are even numbers. Three and seven are odd numbers.

Even also means the same. At half-time in the football match the score was even. Both teams had scored two goals.

Even means flat and level. Mr Slow made the bumpy road even by driving his steamroller over it.

evening

The part of the day between afternoon and night is called the evening. In the evening it begins to get dark.

eventually

Eventually means at last. The farmer tried for a long time to push his tractor out of the mud. Eventually, with Mr Strong's help, he moved it.

ever

Ever means always. Mr Happy enjoyed his holiday by the sea so much, he wished he could stay there for ever.

Ever also means at any time. Have you ever ridden on an elephant?

every

Every means all. Mr Worry wrote down every problem that worried him. It was a very long list!

exactly

Exactly means completely right. Mr Clever was very pleased with the new books he was given for his birthday. They were exactly what he wanted.

exaggerate

To exaggerate is to say that something is bigger or better than it really is. When it thundered, Mr Jelly said it sounded like an earthquake. He was exaggerating. But then he always does!

example

You use an example to show what something is like. An example of Mr Mischief's bad behaviour was the time he cut off half of Mr Fussy's moustache.

excellent

Excellent means very good indeed. When your teacher says that your work is excellent, you can be very pleased.

except

Except means all but. None of the Mr Men here is wearing a scarf, except Mr Snow.

exciting

Exciting means thrilling and enjoyable. Mr Daydream likes to go on exciting adventures.

excuse

When you excuse someone, you let him off for doing something wrong. Ann's teacher excused her when she was late for school.

An excuse is a reason. Whenever Mr Lazy is late, his excuse is that he fell asleep.

exercise

Exercise means practice or activity that keeps you fit. Mr Rush gets plenty of exercise rushing around all day.

exhausted

Exhausted means very tired. Mr Small was exhausted after his long walk home from the seaside. All he wanted to do was sleep.

exist

To exist is to be alive or real. Some people believe that ghosts exist.

explore

To explore is to look around a new place to see what is there. Mr Nosey explored a dark cave at the seaside to see what was inside.

extraordinary

Extraordinary means very strange or unusual. Mr Muddle's house looks most extraordinary. The door is half-way up the wall and the roof is upside down!

extraordinary

expect

To expect is to wait for something that you believe is going to happen. When he saw the grey clouds, Mr Quiet expected it to rain.

expensive

Expensive means costing a lot of money. Mr Uppity is very rich. He buys the most expensive clothes and eats at the most expensive restaurants.

explain

To explain something is to make it easy to understand. Mr Wrong could not tell the difference between a pig and a dog. So Mr Clever explained it to him.

explode

To explode is to burst with a loud noise. The box of fireworks exploded when someone dropped a match into it. What a silly, dangerous thing to do. Everyone nearby heard the explosion.

extremely

Extremely means very much. Mr Fussy was extremely upset by all the damage Mr Clumsy had done during his stay.

eye

You see with your eyes. There are two of them on your face just above your nose. When you close your eyes, you cover them with your eyelids. Above each of your eyes there is a curve of small hairs called an eyebrow.

face

Your face is the front part of your head. On your face you have two eyes, a nose, a mouth and a chin.

To face something is to look towards it. Mr Quiet is facing Mr Small at the table.

fact

A fact is something real and true. It is a fact that dogs and cats are animals.

factory

A factory is a large building where something is made. Cars and sweets and clothing are made in factories.

fade

To fade is to become pale or lose colour. Coloured material can fade when it has been left in the sunlight for a long time. Blue jeans fade after a lot of washing.

faint

To faint means to lose consciousness. When a person faints he falls to the floor and seems to be asleep. People sometimes faint when they are ill or when they have had a shock.

Faint also means weak or not clear. The writing in the old book had become so faint that it was very difficult to read.

fair

Fair means right or reasonable. It is not fair that Mr Greedy should have all the cakes for tea, when Mr Skinny and Mr Happy haven't had any.

Fair also means a light colour. Fair hair is hair that is golden or very light brown. Is your hair dark or fair?

A fair is a place where you can have fun on the amusements such as the dodgems, big dipper and roundabouts. A fair is always outside.

fall

To fall is to drop to a lower place. Mr Bump went shopping on a frosty day and fell over twice before he reached his front gate! By the time he got to the shops he had fallen down eight times!

false

False means not real or not true. You can buy a false beard to wear when you are dressing up or acting in a play.

family

A family is a group of people who are related. Your family includes your parents, brothers and sisters, cousins, aunts and uncles, and grandparents.

famous

Famous means well-known. A crowd gathered to see the famous television star who had come to open the new shop.

far

Far means a long way. Mr Lazy does not like to walk very far. He gets tired just walking to the front gate and back.

fare

The fare is the amount of money you pay to travel on a bus or train.

farm

A farm is land where animals such as cows and pigs are kept. Food like corn and vegetables are grown on a farm.

A farmer is a person who owns or runs a farm. He lives in a farmhouse.

fashion

Fashion means the newest style of clothes or the newest way of doing something. Fashions in women's clothes are different every year. But some girls just wear jeans all the time. Jeans are always fashionable.

fast

Fast means moving at great speed. Mr Rush moves so fast that he can go to the shops and back again in half a minute! It takes Mr Slow all day.

fat

Fat means big all over. Mr Greedy is fat because he eats too much.

Fat is also part of meat. It can be used for cooking.

fault

If something is a person's fault, it means that he is to blame for what has happened. Mr Tickle tickled Mr Dizzy and made him drop a plate. It was Mr Tickle's fault that the plate was broken.

favourite

Your favourite is the one you like the best. Mr Mean's favourite way of spending an afternoon is counting his gold coins.

fear

Fear is a feeling of being very frightened or in danger. Mr Jelly trembled with fear when he heard footsteps outside his house. But it was Mr Happy who had come to visit him.

feast

A feast is a large meal for a special occasion. Mr Greedy dreamt that he was invited to a great feast. There was a long table spread with every kind of food he could think of.

feast

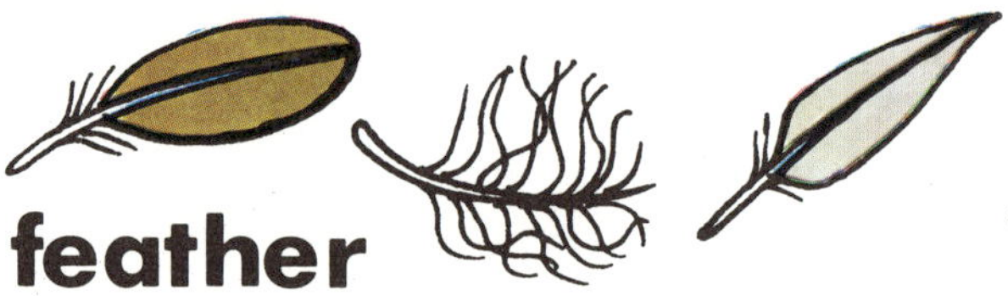

feather

Feathers grow on birds to keep them warm and dry. Feathers are light and fluffy and some are brightly coloured with patterns on them. Small feathers are used to fill cushions and quilts.

feed

To feed is to give a person or an animal food. Mr Muddle was feeding his neighbour's pets while they were on holiday. He fed birdseed to the cat and catfood to the parrot. What a muddle!

feel

To feel is to touch something and know that you have touched it. A kitten feels soft and warm. A frog feels cold and wet.

To feel also means to have a sense of being something. Mr Dizzy felt very upset because everyone laughed at his stupid mistakes.

A feeling is something that you feel. Happiness and anger and fear and worry are all feelings.

female

A female is one that gives birth to young. A female person is a girl or a woman. Some female animals are hens, mares and cows.

fence

A fence is a row of posts and rails or wires. It marks the edge of a piece of ground, such as a garden. A fence around a field is used to keep the animals in.

ferocious

A ferocious animal is very fierce and may bite you. When Mr Jelly heard a tramp snoring in the grass he thought it was a huge ferocious lion.

ferry

A ferry is a boat used to carry people or goods across a narrow stretch of water. Mr Slow likes travelling on a ferry boat because it goes so slowly.

ferry

fetch

To fetch means to go and get something and bring it back. Mr Small couldn't reach the top shelf of his bookcase, so he fetched a ladder.

few

A few means a small number or not many. By the time Mr Greedy had done his shopping at the baker's shop, there were only a few buns and two loaves left!

field

A field is a large piece of land. A farmer usually has several fields where he grows crops and keeps his cows and sheep.

fierce

Fierce means violent or very angry. A fierce animal is one that is likely to attack people. Tigers and bears are fierce animals.

fight

To fight means to hurt a person by hitting him or using a weapon against him. When children fight they hit and wrestle with each other. When soldiers fight in a war they use bombs and guns to kill each other.

fill

To fill means to put something into a container until there is no more room inside. Mr Muddle filled the teapot with milk and the milk jug with lemonade. Oh, Mr Muddle!

film

A film is a story told in moving pictures. At the cinema or on television, films are shown on a screen. Mr Funny likes watching cartoon films.

A film is also a thin strip of material that you put into a camera to take photographs.

filthy

Filthy means very dirty. Mr Messy's kitchen is filthy. He hasn't cleaned the floor for a month and the sink is full of dirty dishes.

finally

Finally means in the end or at last. After hunting all over the house, Mr Muddle finally found his slippers. In the food cupboard!

find

To find means to come across something. Mr Forgetful couldn't find his hat anywhere. He should have looked on his head. He would have found it there!

fine

Fine means well or in good order. Mr Slow was tired after a long walk with Mr Busy. But after a rest he felt fine again.

Fine weather is dry sunny weather. We can have a picnic tomorrow if it is fine.

finger

Your fingers are at the end of your hands. Most people have four fingers and a thumb on each hand. Mr Clumsy's finger was very sore after he hit it with a hammer.

finger

finish

To finish means to bring to an end. After Mr Busy had finished cleaning the kitchen he started working in the garden.

fire

Fire is the heat and light given off by something that is burning. Fire is very hot and will burn you if you touch it.

firm

Firm means solid and not easily moved. Mr Clever made sure that the chair was firm and steady before he stood on it.

first

First means before all the others. The first word this dictionary tells you about is "able".

fish

Fish are cold-blooded animals that live in water. They breathe through gills and have fins and a tail to help them swim. Their bodies are covered in scales.

fit

To fit is to be the right size and shape. Mr Funny's new hat didn't fit very well. It came down over his eyes.

Fit also means well and strong.

fix

To fix means to mend. Mr Clever fixed the alarm clock after he had dropped it on the floor.

To fix also means to attach firmly. The vicar fixed a notice to the door advertising the church fete.

flag

A flag is a piece of material that can be fixed to a pole. Flags have different colours or designs to show that they belong to a country or a group of people.

flame

A flame is fire that shoots up when something is burning. Flames leapt up around the logs after the fire had been lit.

flash

A flash is a sudden bright light. It goes very quickly. After a flash of lightning, thunder soon follows.

To flash is to move very quickly. The motorbikes flashed past as they came round the race track.

flat

A flat surface is smooth and level. Where the countryside is flat, there are no hills.

A flat is a home on one floor of a building. A block of flats may have several floors, with different homes on each one.

flavour

A flavour is a taste. The shop sells three flavours of ice cream. They are chocolate, vanilla and lemon.

flee

To flee is to run away. The thief fled when the policeman came round the corner.

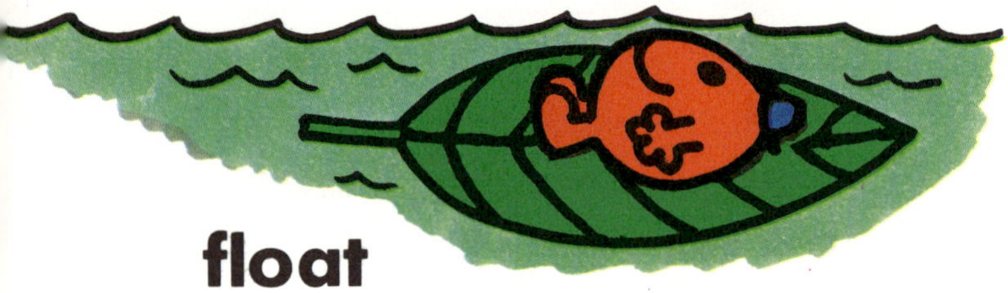

float

To float means to stay on the top of a liquid without sinking. Wood floats on water, but stones sink straight to the bottom.

To float also means to move along gently through the air. When you drop a feather it floats slowly to the ground.

flood

To flood is to fill with too much water. After the rainy weather the river came over the top of its banks and flooded the village.

A flood is an unexpected overflow of water. Many houses were damaged during the floods last spring.

floor

The floor is the part of a room that you walk on. People put rugs or carpets on the floor to make it softer.

flour

Flour is a white or brown powder that is made from ground wheat. Flour is used to make bread and cakes.

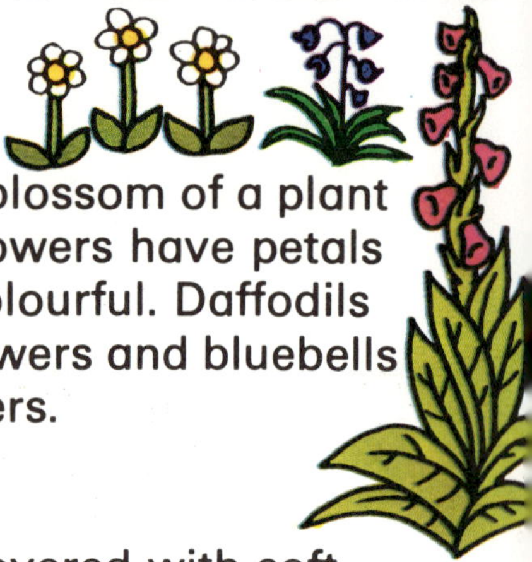

flower

A flower is the blossom of a plant or tree. Most flowers have petals and are very colourful. Daffodils have yellow flowers and bluebells have blue flowers.

fluffy

Fluffy means covered with soft, light hairs or feathers. Baby animals are usually fluffy.

fly

To fly is to move through the air. Birds use their wings to make them fly. An aeroplane has powerful engines to make it fly.

A fly is an insect that flies. There are many different kinds of flies, and most of them are pests. House flies carry disease, and horseflies bite.

foam

Foam is a lot of bubbles on the top of water. Some kinds of soap turn into foam when you swish them around in the bath.

foam

fog

fog

Fog is cloud that has come right down to the ground. Fog makes everywhere look misty. When it is foggy it is hard to see very far.

fold

To fold something is to bend one part on to another part. You fold a letter to fit it into an envelope. Mr Fussy always folds his clothes neatly before he puts them away.

follow

To follow means to go after. Mr Forgetful couldn't remember the way to the shops so he followed Mr Wrong. They ended up at the station!

fond

Fond means liking very much. Mr Mischief is fond of playing tricks on people. Christopher's mother is fond of him, even though he is often naughty.

foolish

Foolish means not sensible. It is foolish to go out in the snow without rubber boots on.

foot

Your foot is the part of your body that is at the end of your leg. You have two feet to stand on.

The foot means the bottom end of something. Mr Small hangs his hat at the foot of his bed.

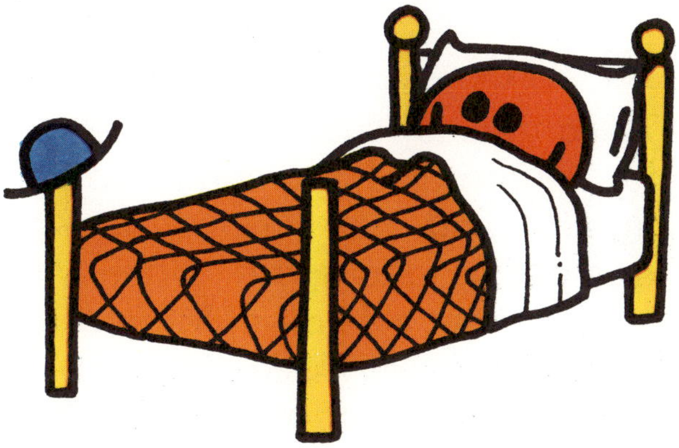

force

Force means making something happen by using strength. Mr Strong forced the door open even though it was locked.

To force also means to make someone do something, even if he doesn't want to. Mr Rush was forced to stand still in the crowded shop. There were so many people, he couldn't move!

forehead

Your forehead is the part of your face above your eyes.

foreign

Foreign means coming from a different country. Some people collect foreign coins as a hobby.

forest

A forest is a large area of land covered with trees.

forget

Forget means not remember. Mr Forgetful forgot to take any money with him to the shops. But it didn't matter, because he had forgotten what he wanted to buy! He is very forgetful!

forgive

To forgive is to excuse someone for saying or doing something against you. You forgive them and are friends again. When Mr Mischief cut off half of Mr Fussy's moustache, Mr Fussy was very cross. But he forgave Mr Mischief in the end.

fork

A fork is a metal object that has three or four points at one end. You use a fork to put food into your mouth.

fortnight

A fortnight is two weeks.

Mr Greedy is going on holiday for two weeks. He has marked the fortnight he will be away on his calendar.

fortunately

Fortunately means luckily. It started to rain as Mr Happy walked home from the shops. Fortunately, he had just bought himself a new umbrella.

fortune

A fortune is a large sum of money. To make a fortune, you have to work very hard or be very lucky.

Your fortune also means what will happen to you in the future. At the fair, there are gipsies who say that they can tell your fortune. But they are not always right.

forwards

Forwards means facing the way you are going. When you walk forwards you can see what is in front of you.

fox

A fox is a wild animal rather like a small dog. Foxes have a thick reddish-brown fur, a long pointed nose, and a bushy tail. Farmers do not like foxes because they steal chickens.

frame

A frame is what you put round something. You put a frame round a picture. Glass goes inside a window-frame. Mr Busy has a picture of Mr Slow in a brown, wooden frame.

free

Free means not costing anything. Mr Mean goes to see a show only if it is free.

Free also means able to move about as you please. Mr Worry felt sorry for the monkeys in their cage at the zoo. He wished he could set them all free.

freeze

To freeze is to become hard or solid because of the cold. One icy winter's morning, Mr Sneeze got up to find that his milk had frozen inside the bottle.

fresh

Fresh means new and not stale. Fresh bread is soft on the inside and crusty on the outside.

friend

A friend is someone who likes you. Mr Silly and Mr Nonsense are great friends. They often visit each other.

frighten

When you frighten someone you make him afraid. Mr Mischief frightened Mr Jelly by jumping out on him from behind a wall.

front

The front of something is the first part or the part that faces forwards. Mr Small has to sit in the front row at the theatre so that he can see the show.

frown

To frown is to wrinkle your forehead. You frown when you are angry or worried or thinking hard. Mr Worry is always frowning. He has wrinkles all over his forehead.

fruit

A fruit is the part of a plant or tree that holds the seeds. Many kinds of fruit are good to eat, like apples and oranges and bananas.

fry

To fry something is to cook it in hot fat or oil. Fish and chips are fried in hot fat.

full

Full means having so much inside that there is no room for any more. The bus conductor wouldn't let anyone else on the bus because it was full.

fun

Fun means amusement. You enjoy something that is fun to do. Mr Tickle had great fun in the park. He tickled everyone in sight!

funny

Something that is funny makes you laugh. Mr Funny wears a funny hat and pulls funny faces to cheer people up.

fur

Fur is thick soft hair. Most mammals have fur covering the whole of their bodies.

furious

Furious means very angry. Mr Uppity was furious when he found that someone had scratched his brand new car.

furniture

Furniture is all the movable things in a house. People use furniture to sit on and put things in or on. Tables, desks, chairs, beds and cupboards are all furniture.

further

further

Further means a greater distance. Mr Chatterbox walked down to the garden gate but Mr Noisy walked further. He walked down to the post office.

fussy

A fussy person likes everything to be clean and tidy. Mr Fussy is so fussy, he even dusts the flowers in his garden!

future

The future is the time that is to come. Nobody knows for certain what will happen in the future.

In future means from now on. A wizard made Mr Mean's nose turn into a carrot when he was mean. Mr Mean decided to be a bit more generous in future.

game

A game is an activity played with a set of rules. A game is played for fun. Football and tennis are ball games, played out of doors. Chess and draughts are board games that can be played indoors.

gang

A gang is a group of people who go around together. There were five boys and two girls in our gang.

gap

A gap is a narrow opening. The dog escaped from the garden through a gap in the hedge.

garage

A garage is a small building near a house where a car is kept.

A garage is also a place where people take their cars to be repaired or to fill them up with petrol.

garage

garden

A garden is the land at the front or back of a house. People grow flowers and vegetables in their gardens and often have a lawn in the middle.

gas

Gas is a fuel used to provide heat in cookers and fires. It is like air, but can be burned to give off heat.

Gas also means a substance that is neither liquid nor solid. The air that we breathe is made up of several gases, including oxygen and nitrogen.

gasp

To gasp is to take a quick short breath. Mr Happy gasped with amazement to see Mr Impossible walking up the side of a house.

gate

A gate is like a door in a fence, a hedge or a wall. Gates are usually made of wood or iron. Mr Topsy Turvy fixed a new gate to his fence. Upside down, of course!

gather

To gather means to collect. In the autumn squirrels gather nuts and hide them ready to eat in the cold winter.

gather

gaze

To gaze at something is to stare at it because you like or admire it or because you are surprised. Some boys were gazing at the toys in the toyshop window. They wanted to buy all of them!

generally

Generally means usually. Mr Busy generally does all his housework before breakfast.

generous

Generous means willing to share what you have with others. My friend is very generous. When she has a bag of sweets she gives one to all her friends.

gentle

Gentle means kind and careful. The boy stroked the cat gently and it began to purr.

ghost

A ghost is the spirit of a dead person. Some people say that ghosts appear in the place where the person once lived.

giant

A giant is a huge, very strong person.You read about giants in stories. Mr Greedy met a giant who punished him for being greedy by making him eat the most gigantic meal.

giant

gigantic

Gigantic means very big, like a giant.

giggle

To giggle is to laugh in a silly way. Mr Mischief giggled when he thought about Mr Funny putting on a hat filled with treacle.

giraffe

giraffe

A giraffe is an animal that lives in Africa. A giraffe has a very long neck, long thin legs and brown patches on its body.
Because it has such a long neck, a giraffe can eat the leaves at the top of trees.

give

To give means to hand something over to another person to keep. Mr Mean was very generous last year. He gave his brother two pieces of coal for Christmas! The year before, he had given him only one piece.

glad

Glad means happy or pleased. Mr Chatterbox is always glad to see people. He likes having someone to talk to.

glare

To glare is to look at someone angrily. Everyone in the library glared at Mr Noisy when he came in talking loudly.

glass

Glass is a hard material that you can see through. Glass breaks easily. It is used for making windows, bottles and drinking glasses.

glasses

Glasses are worn by people to help them see better. They are made of two pieces of glass called lenses. Mr Clever wears glasses.

glasses

gloomy

Gloomy means not cheerful. Nobody can be gloomy for long when Mr Happy is around. He cheers everyone up.

glove

Gloves are clothes you wear on your hands. Gloves fit closely and keep your hands warm. Most gloves are made of leather or wool. Mr Nonsense wears blue gloves.

glow

To glow is to shine. The lights on the Christmas tree are glowing brightly in the dark.

glue

Glue is a substance used to stick things together. Mr Clumsy managed to mend his broken vase with glue. But he managed to glue his hands together while he was doing it!

glum

Glum means miserable.
Mr Greedy looked glum. He had just discovered that he had only one loaf of bread left to eat for breakfast!

A goat eats almost anything.
"Mind your washing, Mrs Washer!"

goat

A goat is a mammal. A goat has short horns and a little beard. A nanny goat gives milk that we can drink. A goat eats almost anything!

goblin

A goblin is a small, man-like creature that appears in fairy stories. The King of the Goblins put a spell on Mr Uppity that made him shrink every time he was rude to anyone.

gold

Gold is a yellowish-orange metal. Rings, watches and other jewellery are made of gold. Gold costs a lot of money.

good

Good means not bad. All the children hoped they would have good weather for their holiday.

Good also means well-behaved. Mr Mischief tried to stop playing tricks on people. He managed to be good for three days.

To be good at something means to be able to do it well. Mr Clumsy is very good at breaking things!

goose

A goose is a large bird. It has webbed feet to help it swim. There are many different kinds of geese. Some are wild, and some are kept on farms for food.

goose

government

A government is a group of people who run a country.

grab

To grab means to take hold of something quickly and suddenly. Mr Rush had no time to stop for lunch. He grabbed a biscuit from the cupboard and rushed out again.

graceful

A graceful movement is smooth and pleasant to watch. The ballerina danced gracefully across the stage.

gradually

Gradually means little by little. By putting away one thing at a time, Mr Slow gradually tidied up his living room. It took him two weeks!

grass

Grass is a green plant with leaves that grow in single blades. A lawn is made up of hundreds and thousands of blades of grass.

grateful

Grateful means thankful for someone doing something for you. When Mr Worry decorated his bedroom, he was very grateful for Mr Tall's help in painting the ceiling.

gravy

Gravy is a brown sauce that you pour over meat. It is made from the juices that come from meat while it is cooking.

graze

To graze means to scrape slightly. Mr Bump grazed his hand on the pavement when he fell over.

To graze also means to eat grass. The cows were grazing in the field.

grease

Grease is any oily substance such as fat. After a breakfast of bacon and eggs, you will be left with a greasy plate.

Grease is also a thick oily substance used to make all kinds of machines run smoothly.

greedy

Greedy means wanting a lot of everything, especially food. When Mr Greedy has a bag of sweets he eats them all himself. Which is very greedy.

green

Green is the colour of leaves and grass. It is a mixture of blue and yellow.

greengrocer

A greengrocer is a person who sells fruit and vegetables. When Mr Noisy went shopping at the greengrocer's he asked for "six ripe tomatoes and two juicy pears"! At the top of his voice!

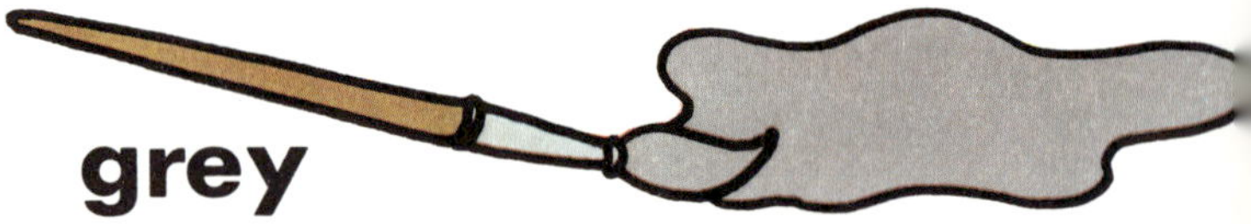

grey

Grey is the colour of the sky on a dark, rainy day when the sun is not shining. If you mix black and white paint together you will make grey.

grin

To grin is to smile. Mr Mischief grins a mischievous grin when he has done something naughty.

grip

To grip is to hold something very tightly. When you climb a tree you must grip the branches firmly so that you do not fall.

groan

To groan is to make a deep moaning sound because you are in pain or unhappy. Poor Mr Lazy groaned when the bus broke down. He had to walk home!

grocer

A grocer is a person who sells things like sugar, biscuits, flour and tins of food.

ground

The ground is the surface of the earth.

The grounds of a building are the gardens and the land around the building.

group

A group is a number of people or things gathered together. Musicians come together to form pop groups.

grow

To grow is to become bigger. John had grown so much in one year that he had to have a completely new set of clothes.

To grow flowers or vegetables is to plant them in the earth and look after them. Last year Mr Busy grew all his own vegetables.

growl

Dogs growl when they are annoyed or are disturbed by a strange noise. They make a deep angry sound in their throats.

grown-up

grown-up

A grown-up is a person who is no longer a child. Your parents and teachers are grown-ups. Another word for a grown-up is an adult.

grumble

To grumble is to complain in a low voice. People usually grumble about things that are not very important. Mr Grumpy always has something to grumble about, even if it is only the weather!

grumpy

Grumpy means bad-tempered. Mr Grumpy is always grumpy. He is rude to everyone he meets.

grunt

To grunt is to make a deep short sound. Pigs grunt. People sometimes grunt when they are annoyed or when they don't want to take any notice. When Mr Happy asked Mr Uppity the time, Mr Uppity just grunted and walked on.

The guard stood on duty outside the palace.

guard

To guard people or things is to watch over them to keep them safe. Some people keep a dog to guard the house.

A guard is a person who watches over or protects someone or something important.

A guard is also a shield that prevents accidents from happening. A fire guard is put in front of a coal fire to stop coals falling out, or people falling in.

guess

When you don't know the right answer to a question you have to guess. A guess may be right or it may be wrong.

guest

A guest is a person who is visiting someone else. Mr Funny invited six guests to his birthday party.

guide

To guide means to lead along or direct. Mr Dizzy lost his way home, so the wizard guided him back along the path.

guilty

If you are guilty it means that you have done something wrong. The thief admitted that he was guilty of stealing the old lady's purse.

gun

A gun is a weapon that fires small pieces of metal called bullets. Guns are used to shoot at a target or to kill animals or people.

gutter

A gutter is a long channel used to drain water away. There are gutters at the sides of roads in towns. There are also gutters on a house to catch the rainwater running off the roof.

gutter

habit

A habit is something you do without thinking because you have done it so often. It is hard to stop a bad habit, like biting your nails.

hair

A hair is a very thin thread. Hair grows on skin. Most people have a mass of hair on their heads. Horses have hair all over their bodies.

half

Half is what you get when you divide something into two parts of the same size. Each part is a half.

Mr Small cut the cucumber in half.

hall

A hall is a large room where people gather for shows or exhibitions or concerts. The school hall was packed on the day of the Nativity play.

A hall is also a corridor or a room just inside the front door o1 a house.

hammer

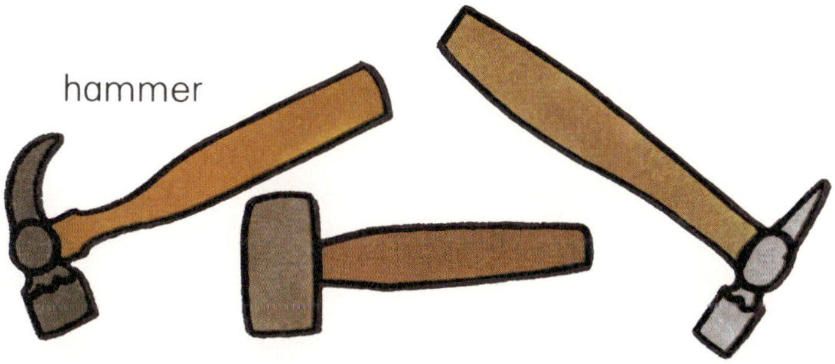

hammer

A hammer is a tool with a heavy metal head. It is used to knock nails into wood. Mr Strong doesn't need a hammer. He can knock nails into the wall just by tapping them with his finger.

hand

Your hands are at the end of your arms. Each hand has four fingers and a thumb. People hold things in their hands.

A hand is also either of the two pointers on a clock. Clocks have a big hand and a small hand.

handkerchief

A handkerchief is a small piece of cloth. You blow your nose on a handkerchief. Mr Messy used his handkerchief to wipe up the jam he had spilt on the table. Then he put it back into his pocket!

handle

The handle of an object is the part you hold it by. Mr Clumsy broke the handle off his teapot when he tried to pick it up.

handy

Handy means useful. Mr Silly finds the handle of his kitchen door handy. He hangs his pork sausages on it!

Handy also means within easy reach. If you have a pen handy, you can write down the shopping list.

hang

When you hang something up you fasten it at one end so that the rest of it is free. Mr Busy hangs his washing on the line with pegs.

happen

To happen is to take place. When Mr Skinny heard a crashing noise in the kitchen he rushed to see what had happened. One of his shelves had collapsed and there were broken cups everywhere!

happy

Happy means pleased. People smile and laugh when they are happy. Mr Happy is nearly always happy.

harbour

A harbour is a sheltered piece of water. Boats are kept in a harbour. They are safe there. Everyone waved as the ship sailed out of the harbour.

harbour

hard

Hard means difficult to do. Mr Rush finds it very hard to stay in one place for more than a minute!

Hard also means firm and solid. Butter goes very hard when it is kept in the fridge.

harm

To harm is to damage or hurt someone or something. Mr Jelly is afraid of mice. He is afraid they will harm him.

hate

To hate means to dislike very much. Mr Messy hates having a bath. He would rather do anything than wash himself.

haunted

A haunted place is supposed to have ghosts in it. Would you like to spend the night in a haunted house?

hay

Hay is dried grass. It is used as food for farm animals. Hay is stored in barns and in haystacks. Mr Dizzy had fun sliding down the haystacks when he went to help on the farm.

head

Your head is the top part of your body, above your neck. It contains your brain. Your face is the front part of your head.

The head is also the chief person in a group. All schools have a head teacher.

heal

To heal is to get well again. When Sarah fell off her bike she cut her knee. But the cut healed quite quickly.

heap

A heap is a pile of things. The keeper in the park swept up the leaves and left them in a heap.

hear

To hear is to listen to sounds through your ears. Nobody can hear Mr Quiet when he speaks because he has such a quiet voice.

heart

Your heart is a very important part of your body. It keeps you alive by pumping blood round your body. If you put your hand on your chest you can feel your heart beating.

hearty

Hearty means jolly and cheerful. Everyone laughed heartily at Mr Funny's jokes.

A hearty meal is a meal that fills you up. We had a hearty lunch after playing outside all morning.

heat

Heat is hotness. It is the opposite of cold. It is nice to sit in the sun in the heat of a summer's day.

heavy

Heavy means weighing a lot. Mr Topsy Turvy's suitcase was so heavy that the handle broke when he tried to lift it.

hedge

A hedge is a row of bushes or trees growing so close together that they make a wall. Hedges are placed around the edge of some gardens instead of a fence.

hedgehog

A hedgehog is a small mammal that has sharp spines on its back. When a hedgehog is frightened it rolls itself into a ball so that the spines stick out all round.

hedgehog

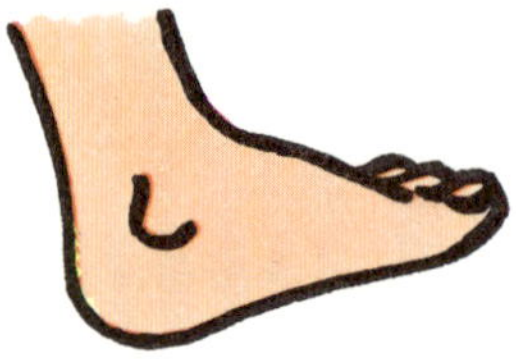

heel

Your heel is the back part of your foot.

height

The height of something is how high or tall it is. Mr Tall doesn't know what his height is because nobody can reach high enough to measure him!

helicopter

A helicopter is a type of aircraft. It does not have wings like an ordinary aeroplane. Instead, it has blades on the top that spin round very quickly and keep it in the air. A helicopter can fly straight up from the ground. It can also stay still in the air.

helicopter

helmet

You wear a helmet to protect your head. People who ride motorbikes have to wear crash helmets. Soldiers and firemen also wear helmets.

help

To help someone is to do something for him when he needs it. Mr Happy helped Mr Miserable to cheer up. He helped him by making him laugh.

hen

A hen is a female chicken. Hens lay eggs that we eat.

herd

A herd is a large group of animals, especially cattle.

hesitate

To hesitate is to wait for a moment before doing something. When he heard his doorbell ring, Mr Jelly hesitated before opening the front door. He was afraid there might be a monster outside!

hide

When you hide something you put it where nobody can see it or find it. Mr Mischief hid Mr Fussy's shoes in the bookcase. Mr Fussy was not very pleased.

high

Something that is high is a long way up from the ground. Mr Tall is so tall he can reach the apples at the top of the highest apple tree without a ladder.

hill

hill

A hill is a piece of ground that rises higher than the land around it. It is hard work climbing up a hill, but coming down is easy!

hint

A hint is a clue or a suggestion. When you cannot think of the answer to a question, it helps if someone gives you a hint. But you still have to find the answer yourself.

hippopotamus

A hippopotamus is a large heavy mammal that lives beside muddy rivers and pools in Africa. It likes to lie in the water with only its nose, eyes and ears showing. A hippopotamus has a thick loose skin with no hair.

hippopotamus

hiss

To hiss is to make a sound like SSSSS! Snakes hiss when they are cross.

hobby

A hobby is something you enjoy doing in your spare time. Some people collect stamps as a hobby, others go fishing or play a musical instrument.

hole

A hole is a space in something. Mr Clumsy burnt a hole in his handkerchief when he was ironing it.

holiday

A holiday is a time when you do not work or go to school. Most people have a short holiday at Christmas. In the summer, people often have a holiday at the seaside or in the country.

hollow

Hollow means having a hole running through the middle of something or having nothing inside. A straw is hollow and you can suck liquid up through it.

home

Your home is the place where you live. For most people, home is a house or a flat, but circus people usually have a caravan for a home.

homework

Homework is work that teachers give children to do at home in the evenings or at the weekend.

honest

Honest means always telling the truth, and not stealing things or cheating.

honey

Honey is a sweet thick liquid made by bees. The bees collect nectar from flowers and make it into honey. You can spread honey on bread and buns.

hop

To hop is to jump up and down on one leg. When Mr Funny lost one of his shoes in the mud, he had to hop all the way home!

hope

To hope is to want something to happen. Mr Small hoped that lots of people would come to his party.

horn

A horn is something that makes a loud noise as a warning. The driver of the car sounded his horn when the child ran into the road.

Horns grow on the heads of certain animals, such as bulls, rams and deer. Horns are hard and pointed. Rhinoceroses have only one horn.

A horn is also a type of musical instrument.

horrible

Horrible means not pleasant at all. Mr Wrong's cakes tasted horrible. He had used salt instead of sugar and washing powder instead of flour. Ugh! How horrid!

horse

A horse is a large mammal. You can ride a horse. Some breeds of horses are used to pull carts. Race horses are specially trained to run in races.

hosepipe

A hosepipe is a long thin tube used to carry water from a tap to another place. You can use a hosepipe to water the garden or to wash a car. Firemen use a big hosepipe for putting out fires.

hospital

A hospital is a place where sick or injured people are looked after. Doctors and nurses work in a hospital, trying to make people well again.

hotel

A hotel is a place where people can stay when they are on holiday or visiting a town far from home. You pay to sleep and eat in a hotel. A large hotel has hundreds of bedrooms.

hour

An hour is a length of time. It is a period of 60 minutes. There are 24 hours in a day. It takes Mr Slow two hours to clean his teeth!

house

A house is a building where people live. Houses usually have two or three floors. A house which has only one floor is called a bungalow.

huge

Huge means very big indeed. This ship looks huge beside the tiny rowing boat.

human

Human means to do with people, not animals. Men and women and children are human, but dogs and cats are not.

hungry

Hungry means wanting to eat. Mr Greedy is always hungry. Even when he has just finished a meal!

hunt

To hunt for something means to look for it everywhere. Mr Messy was hunting for a pencil. His room was so untidy that he had to hunt for a long time!

To hunt animals is to chase them and kill them for food.

hurry

To hurry is to move as quickly as you can. Mr Rush is always in a hurry to get somewhere. He never does anything slowly.

hurt

To hurt means to be painful. Mr Bump tripped over a large stone. His foot hurt for days afterwards.

To hurt also means to do harm to something or somebody.

hymn

A hymn is a song about God. People sing hymns in church and in a school assembly.

ice

Ice is frozen water. It is very slippery and cold. People skate on ice in winter.

ice cream

Ice cream is a cold, sweet food made from frozen cream or fats. It is sometimes flavoured with chocolate or strawberry or mint. Ice cream is good to eat on a hot day.

idea

An idea is something you think of. When his car ran out of petrol, Mr Funny had an idea. He asked Mr Strong to carry his car to the garage. That was a good idea!

idle

Idle means lazy and doing nothing. Mr Lazy is idle for most of the day.

Mr Lazy is idle. He likes to sleep all day and not do any work.

ignorant

Ignorant means knowing very little.

ignore

To ignore someone is to pretend you haven't seen or heard him. Mr Uppity ignored Mr Happy when he met him in the street. He walked straight past without even saying, "Good morning".

ill

Being ill means not feeling well. People stay in bed when they are ill.

When you are ill you have an illness. Mumps and measles are illnesses.

illustration

An illustration is a picture in a book or magazine. Illustrations are used in storybooks to show the reader what something in the story looks like. In this book, illustrations are used to show you what the words mean.

imagine

To imagine something is to picture it in your mind. Imagine what it would really be like to live on a desert island!

imitate

To imitate someone is to copy the way that he speaks or acts. Peter tried to imitate the clown at the circus by pulling funny faces.

immediately

Immediately means straight away. The whistle was blown and the game started immediately.

impatient

Impatient means not wanting to wait. Mr Grumpy is very impatient. He gets annoyed if he has to wait in a queue for more than half a minute.

important

If something is important to you, you care about it very much. Your birthday is an important day for you.

If someone feels important he thinks that people should take a lot of notice of him. Mr Uppity always feels important.

impossible

Something that is impossible cannot be done. Mr Impossible jumped over a house. Nothing is impossible for Mr Impossible!

improve

To improve something is to make it better. Tom worked very hard to improve his handwriting. After two weeks, his teacher told him it had improved so much, she could actually read it!

include

To include means to think of something as part of the whole. The price of our holiday included the plane fare and the hotel.

Including means being part of a group. Including Mr Skinny, there are four Mr Men sitting in the cafe. Excluding him, there are only three.

indeed

Indeed means really. Mr Bounce is quite small but Mr Small is very small indeed.

indigestion

Indigestion is a pain people get when they have eaten too much food too quickly.

indignant

Indignant means cross about something that you feel is unfair or wrong. Mr Chatterbox was most indignant when someone told him he talked too much.

indoors

Indoors means inside a building. You have to play indoors when it is raining.

infectious

An infectious disease is one that is passed on from one person to another. William caught measles from Matthew just by sitting near him. Measles is very infectious!

influence

Influence is the power that one person has over another. If your teacher says that one of your friends is a good influence on you, she means that she thinks he will help you and give you good advice.

information

Information means facts about something or somebody. You can use the books in the library to find out information about many different things.

initials

A person's initials are made up of the first letter of each of his names. Roger Hargreaves' initials are R. H. What are your initials?

injure

To injure means to hurt. Two people were injured in the car accident. One had a broken arm and the other had a leg injury.

innocent

Innocent means not guilty. The young man insisted that he was innocent. He proved his innocence by showing that he had been miles away from the bank when it was robbed.

insect

An insect is a small animal that has six legs. Most insects have wings and can fly. Many insects have two pairs of wings. Beetles and ladybirds and flies are all insects.

inside

Inside means in. Mr Chatterbox keeps his new hat inside a hat box.

insist

To insist is to say something very firmly. Mr Fussy always insists that his guests take off their shoes before they walk on his carpet.

inspect

To inspect something means to look at it closely to check that it is all right. After Mr Messy had done the washing up, Mr Fussy inspected all the plates to make sure that they were properly clean.

instantly

Instantly means at once. The lights went out instantly when the switch was pressed.

instead

Instead means in the place of. Mr Wrong wears a flowerpot on his head instead of a hat.

instruction

An instruction tells you how to do something. When you are making a model from a kit you have to follow the instructions carefully.

instrument

An instrument is an object used for a particular job. A doctor uses instruments when he is operating on a patient.

A musical instrument is used to play music. Recorders and guitars and trumpets are all musical instruments.

insult

To insult someone is to say something rude or hurtful to him. The woman was insulted when someone said her dress looked old-fashioned.

intelligent

Intelligent means clever and using common sense. A sheep dog is very intelligent. It can be trained to look after sheep.

intend

To intend to do something is to plan to do it. Mr Slow intended to finish his book before he went to bed. But he read only two pages. In three hours!

interesting

Something that is interesting makes you want to know more about it because you enjoy it. Mr Chatterbox was watching a film. It was so interesting, he actually stopped talking to listen to it!

Mr Nosey likes to interfere in matters that do not concern him.

interfere

To interfere is to meddle with things that are not your business. Mr Nosey interfered when he overheard two people arguing. He tried to find out what they were arguing about. Nosey people are always interfering like that!

To interfere with means to disturb or get in the way of something. The noise of the television interfered with Tom's homework. He didn't do it very well.

interrupt

To interrupt is to break in on or stop a person who is in the middle of doing something. Mr Lazy's sleep was interrupted by a knock at the door. It was Mr Noisy, coming to wake him up!

invent

To invent means to make something for the first time. Mr Clever invented a toaster that not only toasted the bread, but spread it with butter and marmalade too. What a useful invention!

investigate

To investigate something is to try to find out more about it. When Mr Happy heard a noise in his garden, he went outside to investigate. It was a cat jumping on to the fence.

invisible

Something that is invisible cannot be seen.It is impossible to make yourself invisible, unless you are Mr Impossible!

invite

To invite someone is to ask him to come. Mr Forgetful invited five friends to his party. He wrote out the invitations very carefully, but he forgot to post them!

Mr Fussy likes to iron his clothes very carefully.

iron

An iron is a heavy metal object with one flat side. You heat an iron and use it to press clothes. Most irons are heated by electricity.

Iron is a strong grey metal. Steel is made from iron.

island

An island is a piece of land with water all round it.

island

itch

An itch is a tickling feeling in your skin that makes you want to scratch it. The spots on Alan's arm were very itchy, but the doctor told him he must not scratch them.

jacket

A jacket is a short coat.

jail

A jail is a place where people who have done something wrong are locked up. Jail is also called prison.

jail

jam

Jam is a sweet food made from boiled fruit and sugar. You spread jam on bread or cakes.

To jam means to become stuck or caught. When a door jams, it sticks fast so that it cannot be opened. In a traffic jam, there are so many cars on the road that none of them can move.

jar

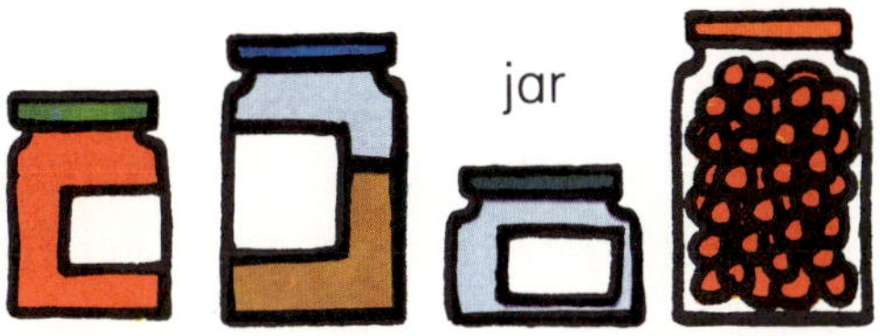

jar

A jar is a round glass object used to hold things. It has a wide opening at the top. Jam is usually sold in jars.

jaw

Your jaws are the bones around your mouth. They hold your teeth. When you open your mouth, your bottom jaw moves down.

jealous

Jealous means wanting something that another person has. The man felt jealous when he saw his neighbour's new car. He wanted one just the same but he knew he couldn't afford to buy one.

jelly

Jelly is a sweet food made from fruit juice and sugar. You can see through jelly and it trembles when you shake it.

Mr Jelly is called Mr Jelly because he trembles like a jelly at the least little thing. He is even frightened of falling leaves!

jet

A jet engine is used to drive an aeroplane. The plane is pushed forward by a jet of hot gas being forced out behind. Planes with these engines are called jets.

A jet is a fast-moving thin stream of liquid or gas. A jet of water shot out of the hosepipe after the tap was turned full on.

jewel

A jewel is a valuable stone that is used to decorate rings and necklaces. Both diamonds and emeralds are jewels.

jewellery

Necklaces, rings, bracelets and brooches are all pieces of jewellery. Some women like to wear a lot of jewellery when they go to a party.

jigsaw

A jigsaw is a kind of puzzle. It is made up of small pieces of odd-shaped cardboard or wood. The pieces fit together to make a picture.

job

A job is the work that someone does to earn a living. Mr Quiet found a job in a library. His job was to look after the books.

join

To join is to fasten two or more things together. If you break one of your toys, you can sometimes join the pieces together with glue.

To join also means to become a member of. Mr Busy couldn't decide whether to join the swimming club or the sailing club. So he joined both!

joke

A joke is something said or done that is meant to be funny. Mr Funny loves telling jokes. He keeps his friends amused for hours.

jolly

Jolly means cheerful and full of fun. Mr Happy is a jolly person. He is hardly ever angry or sad.

jigsaw

journey
On a journey you travel from one place to another. When he went to visit his cousin, Mr Busy took three books with him to read on the train journey.

joy
Joy means happiness. Mr Sneeze was full of joy when he heard that the wizard could cure his cold.

judge

judge
To judge is to choose the winner in a competition. The King of Nonsenseland was the judge of the Silliest Idea of the Year competition. Guess who won the first prize. Mr Silly, of course!

A judge is also a person who sits in a court of law.

jug
A jug is a container made of china, plastic or glass. It is used to hold liquid. A jug has a handle and a lip to make the liquid easier to pour.

juggle
To juggle is to keep a number of objects in the air at the same time. You throw them up with one hand and catch them as they come down with the other hand. At the circus, one of the jugglers was juggling with six plates at the same time.

juice
Juice is a liquid that can be pressed out of fruits, such as oranges, by squeezing them. You can buy fruit juice in bottles at the supermarket.

jumble
A jumble is a mixture of things. Mr Messy sorted through the jumble in his garden shed to find a spade. It took him ages!

jump
To jump is to leap into the air, usually to get over something. The dog jumped over the fence and ran off down the road.

jungle
A jungle is an area of land in a hot country. It is covered all over with trees and creepers and bushes. Mr Daydream landed in the jungle on one of his many adventures. He met an elephant and a crocodile there.

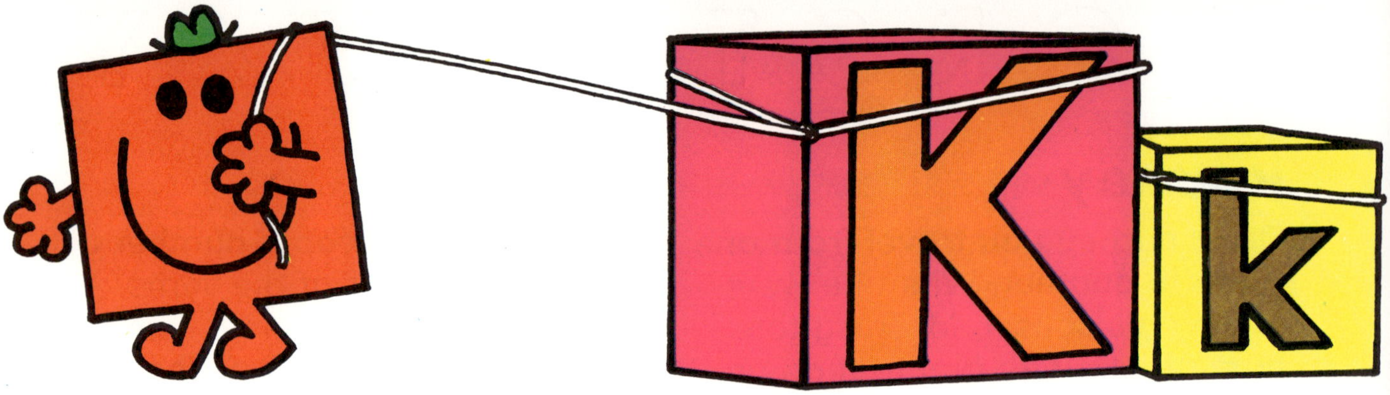

kangaroo

kangaroo

A kangaroo is an animal known as a marsupial. It has a pouch in which it carries its babies. Kangaroos live in Australia. They have two large, strong back legs for hopping and sitting on and two very small front legs or arms.

keep

To keep something is not to give it away or not to get rid of it. Mr Happy said that Mr Clever could keep the book he had borrowed. Mr Happy did not want the book back.

kennel

A kennel is a house for a dog. It is usually made of wood, with a roof and an opening for the dog to get in and out.

kettle

A kettle is a metal pot used to boil water. It has a handle, and a spout to pour the water out.

key

A key is a metal object that is specially shaped to fit a lock. You turn the key in the lock to lock or unlock a door.

keyhole

A keyhole is a small hole in a door where a key fits. Mr Nosey likes to peep through the keyhole to see what is going on inside the room.

Mr Nosey peeps through the keyhole to see what is happening on the other side of the door.

kick

To kick is to hit something or someone with your foot. Mr Strong can kick a football right over a house!

kidnap

To kidnap is to take a person by force and to keep him prisoner until someone else pays the kidnapper money to set him free. When the rich man's son was kidnapped, the kidnapper refused to let the boy go until his father had paid him a lot of money.

kill

To kill a person, animal or plant is to take away its life. The cat was killed when it was hit by a car.

kind

A kind person helps others and is friendly and gentle. Mr Happy kindly offered to help the old lady carry her suitcase. She said he was very kind.

A kind also means a type or a sort. The baker sells many different kinds of cakes.

king

A king is a man who is the head of a country. The country that he is head of is called his kingdom.

kiss

To kiss is to touch someone with your lips. Emma kisses her father and mother every night before she goes to bed.

kit

A kit is a complete collection of things that are needed for a particular job or a hobby. Mr Bump keeps lots of plasters and bandages and cotton wool in his first-aid kit.

kitchen

A kitchen is a room where food is cooked. Mr Fussy's kitchen is always neat and tidy.

Mr Muddle is flying his kite. He has got the string in an awful mess!

kite

You fly a kite. It has a wooden or metal frame, covered with thin cloth, paper or plastic. There is a long string attached to the kite which you hold when you fly it.

kitten

kitten

A kitten is a young cat. A kitten is small and furry and very lovable.

knee

Your knee is the middle part of your leg that bends. Mr Bump nearly always has bruises on his knees from falling over.

knee

kneel

To kneel is to bend your knees so that one knee or both are touching the floor. Mr Clumsy knelt down to pick up the pieces of the plate he had dropped.

knife

A knife is a tool used for cutting. It has a thin sharp blade attached to a handle. There are lots of different kinds of knives. There are pen-knives and kitchen knives and table knives.

knife

knit

To knit is to make clothes like jumpers and scarves by looping wool between two needles. Mr Slow began knitting a pair of socks four years ago. He finished the first one yesterday!

knob

A knob is a small round handle or switch. Doors often have knobs to open them. Mr Clumsy pulled the knob off his radio when he tried to turn it on.

knock

To knock is to rap with your knuckles. The boy knocked on the door of the headmaster's room before he went in.

To knock also means to bump into or move something by accident. Mr Clumsy knocked the cup off the shelf.

knot

A knot is where two pieces of string or rope are tied together. You tie a knot by looping two ends around each other. When Mr Tall's washing line broke, he tied the two ends together in a firm knot.

know

To know is to be sure of something you have learnt or found out. Mr Clever knows the names of all the trees and flowers and animals. But he doesn't know how to find his way home!

knuckle

The bony joints on your fingers are knuckles. You knock on a door with your knuckles.

label

A label is a piece of paper or material that is put on to something to give information. The label on a tin of food tells you what is inside it. The label in your coat shows that it belongs to you.

lace

A lace is a long thin length of cotton or leather used to fasten a shoe. Mr Fussy always irons his shoelaces to keep them looking neat and tidy.

Lace is also a kind of material made from cotton or silk. It has a pattern of holes in it. Mary sewed lace around the collar of her blouse to make it look pretty.

ladder

A ladder is made of two long pieces of wood or metal with shorter pieces, called rungs, in between. You put your feet on the rungs to climb the ladder to reach something high up.

ladybird

A ladybird is an insect that looks like a very small round beetle. It has a red back with black spots on it. You can see ladybirds in the garden.

Mr Bounce tried to climb the ladder. But he kept bouncing off the rungs. Poor Mr Bounce!

lake

A lake is an area of water with land all around it.

lamb

A lamb is a young sheep. Lamb is also the name of the meat we get from lambs.

lamp

A lamp is used to give light. Most lamps have electric bulbs but some are lit by oil. You switch a lamp on when you need light.

land

Land is the dry part of the earth, the part that is not covered by water. A farmer grows crops and keeps animals on his land.

To land is to come back to the ground from the air or from water. The aeroplane landed safely at the airport.

lane

A lane is a small narrow road in the country. Mr Forgetful met some sheep in the lane.

lane

language

Language is the words we use when we speak or write. People from different countries speak different languages. Our language is called English.

lap

Your lap is the flat top part of your legs when you are sitting down. The cat curled up on his master's lap and went to sleep.

large

Large means big. An elephant is large but a mouse is small. A house is larger than an elephant.

larva

A larva is the young form of an insect. A larva looks like a small worm. It hatches from an egg and eats all the time. A caterpillar is the larva of a butterfly.

last

Last means at the end. The last letter of the alphabet is Z.

To last means to go on for a time. You will have to make your pocket money last until next week.

late

Late means coming after the usual or proper time. Mr Slow arranged to meet Mr Busy at six o'clock, but he didn't arrive until eight o'clock. He was two hours late!

laugh

To laugh is to make a sound that shows you are happy. You laugh at something that is funny. Mr Happy laughed and laughed when he saw Mr Muddle trying to sweep the floor with a spade!

laundry

A laundry is a place where clothes and sheets are washed.

Mrs Washer is always busy in the laundry washing clothes.

law

A law is a rule made by a government. All the people in the country must obey the law. A policeman's job is to stop people breaking the law. One of the laws of our country says that we must drive on the left-hand side of the road.

lawn

A lawn is a piece of grass in a garden or a park. The grass is cut with a lawn mower to keep it short and tidy.

lay

To lay is to put down. Mr Fussy laid his jumper carefully in the drawer, so that it would not get creased. A hen lays eggs for us to eat.

To lay the table means to put on the table all the things you need for a meal.

layer

A layer is one thickness of something. Mr Greedy bought a cake that had a layer of chocolate, a layer of vanilla and a layer of strawberry. What a cake!

lazy

A lazy person likes to do nothing. Mr Lazy doesn't like working. He would rather sleep all day.

lead

To lead someone is to show him the way. Once Mr Wrong got hopelessly lost in the wood. But Mr Quiet led him out. Mr Quiet knows the woods well because he lives there.

A lead is a long thin piece of leather. You fix it to a dog's collar when you take the dog for a walk.

lead

Lead is a very heavy metal.

Lead is also the name for the hard black part of a pencil, that makes a mark when you write with it.

leaf

A leaf is part of a tree or plant. Leaves grow in many different shapes and sizes and most of them are green. Daffodils have long thin leaves. In the autumn, the leaves of some trees go brown and fall to the ground. These trees grow new leaves every spring.

leak

To leak is to lose liquid or gas through a hole. Mr Busy took a bucket of water upstairs to clean the windows. But the bucket was leaking. By the time he got upstairs the bucket was empty!

lean

To lean on something is to rest on it or against it. Mr Strong leant against the shed and it collapsed!

leap

leap

To leap is to jump. The horse leapt over the fence and galloped away across the fields.

learn

To learn is to get to know about something or to find out how to do something. Children learn to read and write at school.

leather

Leather is a strong material made from the skin of a dead animal. Shoes and handbags can be made of leather.

leave

To leave is to go away from. Mr Happy had to leave his house very early to catch a train.

To leave also means not to take. Mr Forgetful always leaves something behind.

left

The left is the opposite side to the right. When you read or write you start at the left-hand side of the page and work towards the right.

leg

Legs are limbs for walking on. They are part of your body. You use your two legs when you walk. Mr Tall has very long legs, so he can walk very fast.

lemon

A lemon is a yellow fruit. It has a very sour taste.

lemonade

Lemonade is a drink made from lemon juice, sugar and water.

lend

To lend is to let someone use something that belongs to you for a short time. When you lend someone your pencil you expect to get it back.

length

The length of something is how far it is from one end to the other. You can measure the length of a line by using a ruler.

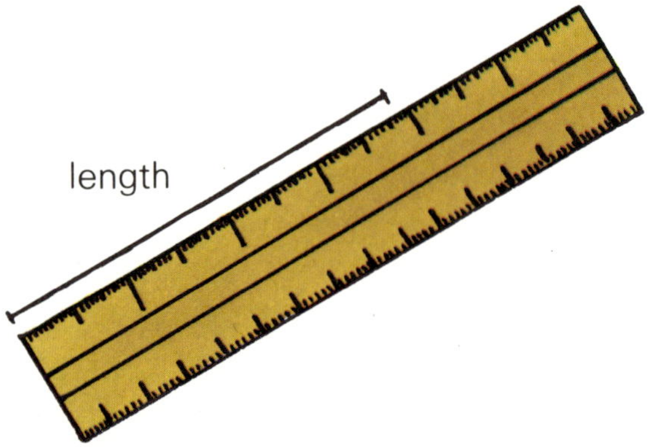

lens

A lens is a piece of curved glass. When you look through it, a lens makes things look bigger or smaller. The glass part of a pair of glasses is called a lens. So is a magnifying glass.

leopard

A leopard is a large fierce animal that has yellow fur with black spots. Leopards are like cats, but they are much bigger. They live in Africa and Asia.

lesson

A lesson is a time when you learn something. We have a swimming lesson on Thursdays.

letter

Letters are used to make up words. The last three letters of the alphabet are XYZ.

A letter is also a message that you write on paper. You put the letter in an envelope and send it to someone.

lettuce

Lettuce is a vegetable. It has large green leaves. You eat lettuce raw in salads.

level

Level means flat and not sloping. Mr Wrong's table was not level, so his plates kept sliding off it!

library

A library is a place where books are kept for people to borrow. You can go to a library when you need a quiet place to read or study.

lick

To lick is to move your tongue over something. She licked the ice cream until it was finished.

lid

A lid is a cover for a box or a tin or a jar. You take off the lid to see what is inside.

lie

To lie is to stretch out flat on the floor or on a bed. The cat likes to lie on the rug in front of the fire.

To lie also means to say something that is not true.

life

Your life is the time when you are alive. The farmer has spent all his life in the same village. He has never lived anywhere else.

lifeboat

A lifeboat is a special kind of boat used to rescue people who are in trouble at sea.

lift

To lift something is to pick it up. Mr Strong can lift a car with no trouble at all.

A lift is used to take people from floor to floor in a tall building. It saves them walking up and down the stairs. A lift has sliding doors, and is hung on metal ropes.

light

Light comes from the sun and from electric lamps and torches. Light makes it possible for us to see. It is light in the daytime and dark at night. Most houses are lit with electric lights when it is dark.

Light also means not heavy. A feather is very light.

lightning

Lightning is a sudden flash of light seen in the sky during a thunderstorm.

like

To like something means to enjoy it. Mr Chatterbox likes talking. It is his favourite way of passing the time.

Like also means nearly the same as. Mr Daydream is like a blue cloud.

limb

A limb is a part of your body. Legs and arms are limbs.

limit

The limit is as far as you can go or as much as you can do. There is a speed limit. Drivers are not allowed to drive their cars faster than the speed limit.

limousine

A limousine is a large expensive car. Mr Uppity is very proud of his limousine.

limousine

limp

To limp is to walk with some difficulty. Mr Bump tripped over a chair and hurt his foot. He was limping for the next few days.

line

A line is a long thin mark. Mr Dizzy cannot draw a straight line, even when he uses a ruler.

A line is also a row of things or people, one behind or beside the other. There was a line of people waiting for the bus.

lion

lion

A lion is a large fierce animal that lives in the jungles of Africa and Asia. Lions are like cats, but they are much bigger. They have yellow fur. A male lion has a lot of hair round its head called a mane.

lip

Your lips are the pink parts around your mouth. Mr Greedy licked his lips as he sat down to his dinner.

liquid

A liquid is anything wet that can be poured. Water and milk are liquids.

list

A list is a number of words or names arranged one below the other. Mr Worry made a list of all the things he had to worry about. It was a very long list indeed!

listen

To listen is to try to hear a sound. You listen with your ears. Mr Nosey pressed his ear against the wall to listen to what was going on in the next room.

litter

Litter is bits of paper and other rubbish that are dropped on the ground. Most parks have litter bins for people to put their rubbish in. They help to keep the park clean and tidy.

litter

little

Little means not big. Mr Small is very little. He is not much bigger than a pin.

live

To live means to be alive and not dead. Fish cannot live out of water.

To live also means to spend your time in a particular place. Mr Funny lives in a teapot!

lizard

lizard

A lizard is a reptile. A lizard has four short legs and a long tail. It likes to sit on rocks or sand in the hot sun.

load

A load is something carried. Lorries carry heavy loads.

loaf

A loaf is bread cooked in one piece. It has a crust all round the outside.

local

Local means to do with the area you live in. Mr Nosey always reads the local newspaper to find out what has been going on in and around Tiddletown.

lock

To lock is to fasten something with a key. Mr Jelly locks all his doors and windows at night.

log

A log is a piece of wood from a tree. Mr Busy likes cutting up logs for his fire.

log

lonely

Lonely means feeling sad because you are not with anyone else and on your own. Mr Small felt very lonely when he first moved into his new house. Nobody came to see him.

long

Long means a great length from end to end. Mr Tickle's arms are very long. He can reach all the way down to the kitchen when he is lying in bed!

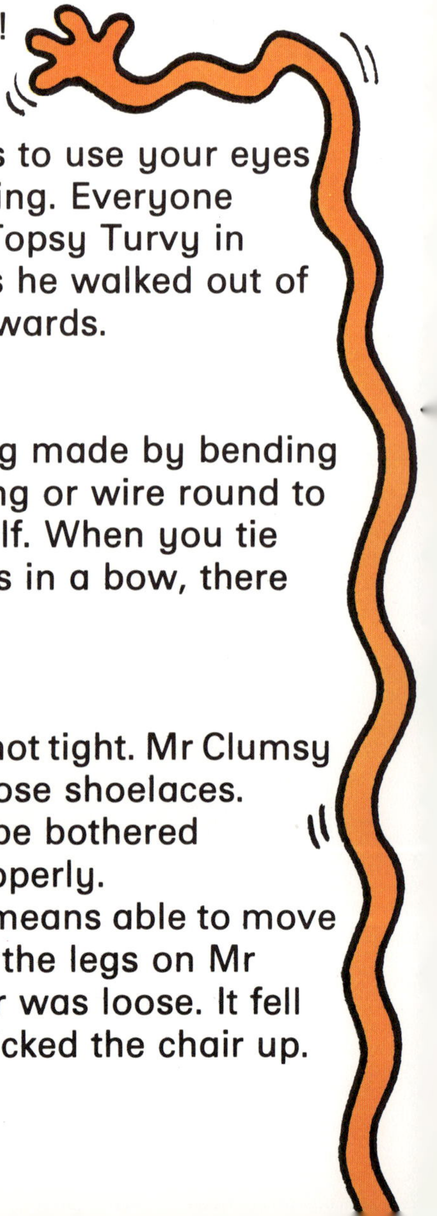

look

To look means to use your eyes to see something. Everyone looked at Mr Topsy Turvy in amazement as he walked out of the shop backwards.

loop

A loop is a ring made by bending a piece of string or wire round to cross over itself. When you tie your shoelaces in a bow, there are two loops.

loose

Loose means not tight. Mr Clumsy always has loose shoelaces. He can never be bothered to tie them properly.

Loose also means able to move easily. One of the legs on Mr Clumsy's chair was loose. It fell off when he picked the chair up.

lorry

lorry

A lorry is a large vehicle used to carry heavy loads. Mr Wrong tried to take a ride on a lorry. He thought it was a bus!

lose

To lose something is to drop it or forget where you have put it. Mr Forgetful loses something every day. Yesterday he lost his hat. He found it eventually on his head!

lot

A lot means many. Mr Happy has a lot of friends because he is such a happy friendly person.

loud

Loud means making a lot of noise or being easily heard. Mr Noisy snores so loudly that he keeps everyone awake for miles around!

love

To love is to like someone or something very much. Karen loves her baby brother.

lovely

Lovely means pleasing or pretty. Ann bought a lovely dress in the shop. She thought it was beautiful.

low

Low means not high. The tree has some low branches. They are very close to the ground.

lucky

A lucky person has good things happen to him by chance. Mr Sneeze thought he was very lucky when the sun shone for the whole of his holiday.

luggage

Luggage is the suitcases and bags that a person carries with him on a journey. When Mr Forgetful went on holiday, he left all his luggage on the train!

lump

A lump is a piece of something. The teacher gave all the children a lump of clay and told them to make an animal with it.

lunch

Lunch is the meal that you have in the middle of the day. Some children stay at school for their lunch, others go home.

machine

A machine is a tool with many parts that does work for us. A sewing machine sews clothes faster and neater than a person can do.

mad

Mad means very silly or crazy. Mr Silly does mad things like putting marmalade in his coffee.

magazine

A magazine contains stories, pictures and information. It has a thin paper cover. Magazines usually come out once a week or once a month.

magic

In stories, magic is a power that witches and fairies and goblins have. The King of the Goblins put a magic spell on Mr Uppity, so that he shrank every time he was rude to anyone.

Magic is about things that seem unreal or impossible. A magician performs magic tricks like pulling a live rabbit out of a hat.

magnet

A magnet is a special piece of metal. It has the power to pull small iron objects towards it.

magnet

mail

Mail is the letters and cards and packages that are sent through the post. The postman delivers mail to your address.

main

Main means the most important. The main reason for going to the park is to feed the swans.

male

Male is the opposite of female. Men are male. Bulls are male animals. Cocks are male chickens.

mammal

A mammal is a warm-blooded animal. The babies of mammals are born alive, not in an egg like birds and reptiles. Female mammals feed their young with milk from their bodies. Most mammals have fur or hair on their bodies. People are mammals, and so are horses and dogs and cats.

mammoth

A mammoth is a very large animal that lived thousands of years ago. Mammoths were like elephants, but with thick fur all over their bodies and two huge, curved tusks.

mammoth

manage

To manage is to succeed in doing something. Mr Small managed to reach the letterbox by standing on a pile of books. He managed to climb up every one. It was hard work!

mane

A mane is a mass of long hair along the neck of a horse or around the head of a male lion.

manners

Manners are a polite way of behaving. Mr Grumpy has no manners at all. He never says "Please" or "Thank you".

many

Many means a large number of. Mr Impossible can do many things that nobody else can do. There are many words in this book.

map

map

A map is a detailed drawing of a town or a country or the world. A map shows the shape of a country and where there are towns, rivers, lakes and mountains.

marble

A marble is a small glass ball used in games. Most marbles have colours inside the glass.

Marble is also a kind of stone that can be polished. Palaces and churches are sometimes built with marble.

march

To march is to walk with regular steps, often in time to music. When soldiers march, they walk in step with each other.

margarine

Margarine is a fat that we eat. It looks like butter and tastes nearly the same. It is made from animal or vegetable oil.

mark

A mark is a small spot or smudge on something. When Mr Messy has been reading a book, there are dirty marks all over the pages from his dirty fingers.

A mark is also a grade or a number that shows how well you have done in a test or a piece of school work.

market

A market is a place where fruit and vegetables and other things are sold on stalls. Some markets are outdoors, others are in a covered area.

marmalade

Marmalade is a thick jam usually made from oranges. It has a slightly bitter taste. Bits of peel are added to give the marmalade more flavour.

marry

When a man and a woman marry they become husband and wife. They promise that they will always love and care for each other.

market

marvellous

Marvellous means wonderful or very good. Mr Silly had a marvellous time at the fair. He enjoyed himself so much, he wanted to go back there again the next day.

mash

To mash is to make something into a soft mass. Mr Fussy does not like to find lumps in his mashed potatoes.

mask

A mask is a covering that you wear over your face or eyes as a disguise. Mr Dizzy is wearing a mask that makes him look like a cat.

master

A master is a man who is in charge of something. The dog soon learned to obey its master.

mat

A mat is a small covering for the floor or a piece of material used to protect something. You wipe your dirty feet on a doormat when you come into the house. Mr Fussy puts table mats on the table so that the hot dishes do not mark it.

match

A match is a small stick of wood or cardboard that makes a flame when it is struck against a matchbox.

A match is also a game played between two sides. In a football match, two teams try to score goals against each other.

To match is to be alike. Mr Wrong's shoes do not match. One is black and the other is brown.

material

Material is anything that is used to make something else. Paper, paints and a paintbrush are the materials you need to paint a picture. Mr Fussy bought some yellow material to make some new curtains for his house.

matter

To matter is to be important. Mr Clumsy broke one of Mr Happy's cups. But Mr Happy said it didn't matter. It was only an old chipped cup.

mattress

A mattress is a large thick pad put on a bed to make it comfortable to sleep on.

maze

A maze is a sort of puzzle. A maze has many paths with high hedges on either side, specially made so that it is difficult to find your way around.

meadow

A meadow is a field of grass. Cows graze in a meadow.

meagre

Meagre means small or not enough. Mr Skinny eats a meagre breakfast. One cornflake. That's all! No wonder he is skinny!

The Mr Men are having a lovely time trying to find their way round this maze.

meal

A meal is the food that you eat at a certain time of the day. Breakfast is the first meal of the day.

mean

What a word means is what it stands for. Small means not very big. It means the same as little.

To mean to do something is to do it on purpose. Mr Clumsy did not mean to break the teapot, it just slipped out of his hand.

Mean also means selfish and not wanting to share things with other people. Mr Mean has a box full of money but he is too mean to spend it.

measles

Measles is a disease. When you have measles your body has red spots all over it and you feel ill. You catch measles from other people.

measure

To measure is to find out how big something is. Mr Busy measured the floor of his bedroom to find out how much carpet he would need.

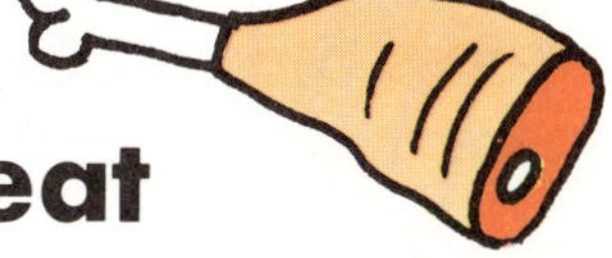

meat

Meat is the flesh of an animal, which is used as food. Pork is meat that comes from a pig.

medal

A medal is a piece of metal like a coin that is given to someone as a prize or because he has done something brave. The team won two gold medals and one silver medal in the swimming contest.

medicine

Medicine is a liquid or pill that the doctor gives you when you are ill. You take the medicine to help you get better.

meet

To meet is to come together with someone. You may meet a person by chance, or you may plan to meet him at a particular time. Mr Happy met Mr Greedy in the sweetshop.

A meeting is a group of people who meet for a special reason. Cub Scouts hold a meeting once a week after school.

melt

To melt is to change from something solid to liquid because of heat. Mr Silly built a snowman. In his living room! It soon melted and left a big puddle of water on the carpet.

member

A member is someone who belongs to something like a club, a group or a church. Only members of the swimming club are allowed to use the pool.

memory

Your memory is the part of your brain that helps you to remember things. Mr Forgetful has a very bad memory. Sometimes he cannot even remember his name!

menace

A menace is someone or something that could cause trouble or danger. The stray dog was a menace to traffic. It ran into the road and nearly caused an accident.

mend

To mend something is to put it together again after it has been broken or torn.

mention

To mention is to speak about. When I talked to Kate's father on the phone, he mentioned that she was going to go to a new school.

menu

A menu is a list of the food that you can choose from in a restaurant or a cafe. Mr Uppity always orders the most expensive things on the menu.

mermaid

A mermaid is a make-believe creature. A mermaid is half woman and half fish, and lives in the sea.

merry

Merry means jolly and full of fun. Mr Busy whistled a merry tune as he did his housework.

mess

A mess is an untidy or dirty muddle.

message

A message is a few words sent from one person to another. Mother sent a message to the teacher to say that Alan was ill and could not go to school.

messenger

A messenger is a person who delivers a message. Mr Forgetful is not much use as a messenger, because he can never remember the message he is supposed to deliver!

messy

Messy means untidy or dirty. Mr Messy never puts things away or cleans his house or weeds his garden. What a messy person!

metal

Metal is a solid such as iron or silver. Many metals have a shiny surface when they are polished. Metal can be melted. It is used to make things like engines and machines and tins.

microphone

A microphone is used to make sounds louder. Pop singers sing into a microphone so that everyone can hear them.

microscope

A microscope is used to see very small things or things that cannot be seen with the eye alone. It has lenses in it that make things look bigger.

middle

The middle of something is its centre. It is the same distance away from all the sides. There is a white line down the middle of most main roads.

midnight

Midnight is 12 o'clock at night.

milk

Milk is a liquid food. We drink milk that comes from cows. Milk comes from female animals. It is used to feed their babies.

mince

To mince is to chop into very small pieces. Meat can be minced to make hamburgers.

mincemeat

Mincemeat is a sweet filling used in mince pies. It is made from raisins, currants, apples, sugar and spices minced together.

mind

To mind is to be upset or annoyed by something. Mr Lazy didn't mind that Mr Slow was an hour late for tea. It meant he could sleep for an hour longer!

To mind also means to look after. The baker asked his assistant to mind the shop while he baked some more bread.

Your mind is the part of your brain that you use to think and learn and remember. To change your mind means to decide to do something different.

mine

Mine means belonging to me. That book is mine.

A mine is a place very deep underground. Miners dig for things like coal and iron in a mine.

mineral

A mineral is a substance that is formed by nature in the ground. Minerals are not animals or plants. Coal and salt and gold are minerals.

mint

Mint is a plant. It is used to make mint sauce to eat with roast lamb. It is also used to flavour sweets and ice cream.

minute

A minute is a length of time. There are 60 seconds in a minute. There are 60 minutes in an hour. Mr Busy can clean his house from top to bottom in five minutes!

All the Mr Men except one are busy in this mine. Which miner is sleeping?

miss

To miss is not to hit or catch something. Mr Clever threw the ball to Mr Clumsy, but Mr Clumsy missed it. It went straight through his neighbour's window.

To miss also means to notice that someone is away, or that something is not there. Jennifer missed her mother while she was staying with her grandmother.

missing

Missing means lost or not here. Mr Mean counts his gold coins every day to make sure that none of them is missing.

mistake

A mistake is something that is wrong. Mr Wrong worked as a waiter in a restaurant. But he had to leave because he kept making mistakes. He kept giving the wrong food to the customers.

mirror

A mirror is a piece of glass with a silver backing. You can see yourself in a mirror. Mr Funny wondered why everyone was laughing at him more than usual. He looked in the mirror and saw that he had his hat on upside down!

mischief

Mischief means bad behaviour. To get up to mischief is to be naughty and to play tricks on people. A mischievous person is always up to mischief, just like Mr Mischief!

miserable

Miserable means not happy or not cheerful. Mr Dizzy was miserable because everyone laughed at the silly things he said.

mix

To mix is to put several different things together. You mix flour and fat together to make pastry.

To mix up means to muddle or confuse. Mr Muddle is always getting things mixed up. For instance, he will say "Good morning" when he should be saying "Good night"!

moan

To moan is to grumble and complain. Mr Grumpy moaned when Mr Happy left the door open, because he felt a draught.

To moan also means to make a low crying sound because you are in pain or unhappy.

model

A model is a person who wears new clothes to show other people what they are like.

A model is also a small exact copy of a larger object. Michael made a model aeroplane from a kit.

modern

Modern means to do with the present time. My grandmother does not like watching modern films on television. She prefers films that were made many years ago, when she was young.

modest

A modest person does not boast about himself or show off. Susan was a modest girl. She did not tell her uncle she was the best swimmer in the class.

mole

A mole is a small mammal with dark velvety fur and a long nose. Moles are a nuisance to gardeners because they make molehills on the lawn.

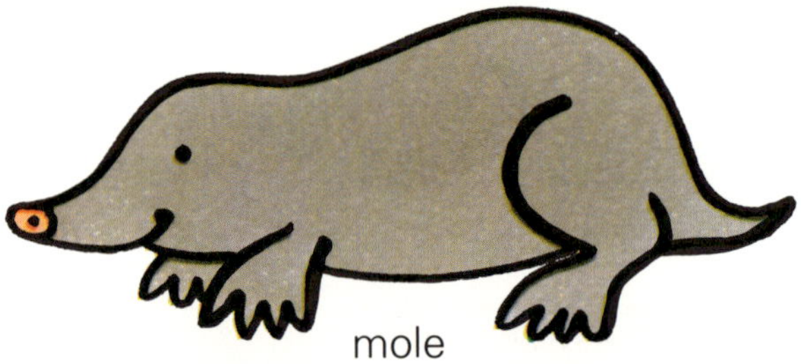

mole

moment

A moment is a very short space of time. You can blink your eyes in a moment. It takes only a moment to say "Hello".

money

Money is the coins and notes we use to buy things and to pay people. Mr Uppity has lots of money. He is the richest person in Bigtown.

monkey

A monkey is a mammal that has hands and feet like a human being. Monkeys are covered with hair and have a long tail. There are many different types of monkey. Some of them are very intelligent and can do tricks.

monocle

A monocle is a glass lens that is worn over just one eye. A monocle helps you to see better. Mr Uppity wears a monocle.

monster

A monster is a large frightening creature. Monsters usually appear in horror stories, but they do not really exist.

month

A month is a length of time. There are 12 months in a year, and each one has a different name. All the months except February are 30 or 31 days long.

mood

A mood is the way that you feel at a particular time. Mr Happy is nearly always in a good mood.

moon

The moon is a satellite of the earth. It moves around the earth and shines in the sky at night.

mop

A mop is a piece of equipment used to clean or polish floors. It has a long handle with a head of soft material at one end.

To mop up is to clean up spilt liquid with a mop or cloth.

morning

The morning is the first half of the day. Morning is the time between midnight and midday. Mr Tickle likes to finish all his work in the morning. Then he can spend the afternoon looking for people to tickle!

moss

Moss is a small green plant that grows on rocks and trees. It looks like a soft green mat.

moth

A moth is an insect that usually flies at night. A moth is like a butterfly but its wings are not so brightly coloured.

motor

A motor makes a machine work. The motor of a car is what makes it go. A motorboat is a boat that is driven by a motor. A motorbike is a bicycle that is driven by a motor.

mountain

A mountain is a piece of land that rises up much higher than the land around it. A mountain is much higher than a hill.

mouse

A mouse is a small furry animal with a long tail. Some mice live in houses and others in fields. Some people keep white mice as pets. Cats and owls like to catch mice and eat them.

moustache

A moustache is the hair that grows on a man's upper lip. Mr Slow has a white moustache.

mouth

Your mouth is part of your face. You can open and close your mouth and you use it to eat, drink and speak.

move

To move is to put something in a different place. Mr Happy moved all his furniture out of the room so that he could paint the walls.

mow

To mow is to cut grass short with a lawn mower. Mr Busy mows his lawn every day.

much

Much means a lot. It rained so much today that deep puddles appeared everywhere.

mud

Mud is soft wet earth. Mr Messy was covered in mud after his walk in the country.

muddle

To muddle is to mix things up by mistake. Mr Muddle sometimes wears his shoes on his hands and his gloves on his feet. What a muddle!

muffle

To muffle a sound is to make it quieter. Mr Mischief wore soft shoes to muffle his footsteps when he went to play a trick on Mr Jelly.

mug

A mug is like a large cup that is used without a saucer. Mr Sneeze has a mug with his name on it.

mug

mumps

Mumps is a disease that you catch from someone else. When you have mumps the sides of your face become swollen and sore.

munch

To munch is to make a noise when you chew something. Mr Greedy munched his way through a plateful of biscuits at teatime.

murder

Murder is killing someone deliberately. Murder is against the law.

muscle

Your muscles are part of the inside of your body. Muscles help you to move and lift and hold things. Mr Strong must have very strong muscles to lift such heavy weights.

museum

museum

A museum is a building where interesting things are on show for people to see. The museum in our town has several dinosaurs.

mushroom

A mushroom is a plant known as fungus. Some mushrooms are shaped like small umbrellas. Mushrooms grow in fields and in damp places, but they are hard to find. You can eat some kinds of mushrooms, but others are poisonous.

music

Music is the sound made by musical instruments and by people when they sing. Jazz, classical and pop are all types of music but there are many more.

Music is also the notes for a particular piece of music, written down for a musician or singer to read.

music

musician

A musician is a person who plays a musical instrument or sings. Violinists, trumpeters and piano players are musicians.

mustard

Mustard is a yellow powder made from the seeds of the mustard plant. Mustard tastes very hot. It is eaten with many meat dishes.

mutter

To mutter is to speak in a low voice, as if you don't want people to hear. Mr Mean muttered about the price of food when he went shopping.

mystery

A mystery is a strange thing that we cannot understand or explain. No one can explain how Mr Impossible can become invisible. It is a mystery.

nail

A nail is a thin round piece of metal with a sharp point at one end. Nails are hammered into pieces of wood to hold the wood together.

A nail is also the hard flat covering at the end of a finger or toe.

name

The name of a person or place is the word he or it is known by. The name of the town where Mr Uppity lives is Bigtown. What is your name?

nap

A nap is a short sleep. Mr Lazy likes to have a nap after his lunch.

narrow

Narrow means not wide. Mr Greedy tried to squeeze through a narrow opening in the fence. But he got stuck because he was so fat!

nasty

Nasty means unpleasant. Tom had a nasty accident on his bike. He fell off and grazed his knee badly.

natural

Natural means made by nature, not by people. Honey is a natural food. Lucy's hair is natural. It is not a wig.

nature

Nature is everything that grows on the earth. It is all the things that cannot be made by man. Flowers and fruit and trees are all provided by nature.

naughty

Naughty means behaving badly. Mr Mischief is naughty. Once he tied Mr Silly's shoelaces together. That was very naughty!

navy

The navy is all the warships that belong to a country and all the sailors who serve in them.

Navy is also a very dark blue colour. Its full name is navy blue.

These three ships and their sailors are all part of one navy.

near

Near means not far away. There is a park near our house where we play. It takes only five minutes to walk there.

nearly

Nearly means almost. Robert has nearly enough money to buy the record he wants. He needs only one more week's pocket money.

neat

Neat means tidy. Mr Fussy writes very carefully and neatly. It is easy to read his writing.

necessary

If something is necessary it is something that you must do or have. It is necessary to buy a ticket in order to travel on the train.

neck

Your neck is the part of your body that joins your head to the top of your shoulders. Mr Snow wears a scarf around his neck.

need

If you need something you must have it. You need a pencil and paper if you want to write a letter.

needle

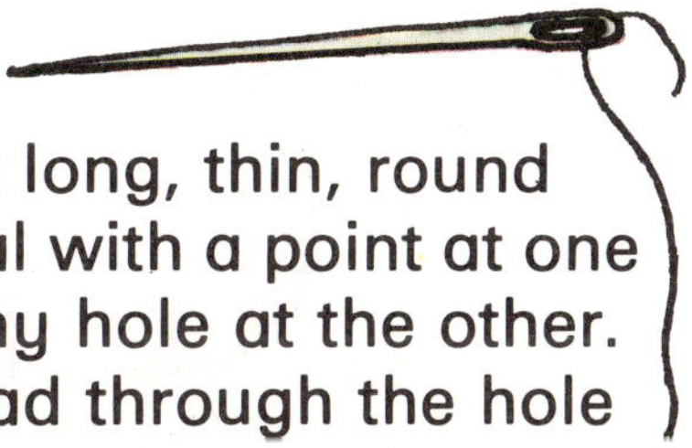

A needle is a long, thin, round piece of metal with a point at one end and a tiny hole at the other. You put thread through the hole and use the needle and thread to join pieces of cloth together.

neglect

To neglect means not to care for or look after. Mr Messy neglects his house. It is full of holes.

neighbour

A neighbour is a person who lives next door to or near you. Mr Nosey always likes to know what his neighbours are doing. Sometimes he peeps through their windows to find out!

neighbourhood

A neighbourhood is a district of a town or city. There is only one shop in the neighbourhood where we live.

neither

Neither means not one or the other. Neither Mr Happy nor Mr Worry wears a hat.

nervous

Nervous means worried about something that is going to happen. Tim is always very nervous before a test at school. He is afraid that he might not know the answers.

nest

A nest is a bird's home. Many birds build their nests out of twigs and grass and mud. Nests are usually built in trees and hedges. Female birds lay their eggs in nests.

net

A net is a piece of loosely made material that has even rows of holes in it. Small nets can be fixed to sticks and used to catch fish in pools. Deep-sea fishermen use huge nets to catch shoals of fish.

never

Never means not ever. Mr Mean never goes on holiday because he says he cannot afford it.

new

New means not old or used. Peter bought a new pair of shoes. His old ones were worn out.

news

News is information about things that have recently happened. Mr Clever listens to the news on the radio every morning to find out what is going on in Cleverland.

newspaper

A newspaper is made up of large printed sheets of paper folded together. A daily newspaper gives information about news, sport, and other interesting things that have happened, usually the day before or very recently.

next

Next means after this. Mr Tickle has just tickled the postman and made him drop all his letters. He is going to tickle the policeman next.

Next to means alongside. The butcher's shop is next to the baker's in the High Street.

nibble

To nibble is to eat something by biting off only a small piece at a time. The hamster nibbled a lettuce leaf.

nickname

A nickname is a name that your friends may use instead of your real name. Joe's nickname is "Ginger" because he has red hair.

nightmare

A nightmare is a very nasty dream. Mr Jelly had a nightmare about being chased by a lion.

nil

Nil means nothing. At half-time, the score in the football match was two–nil. One team hadn't scored any goals at all.

nod

To nod is to move your head up and down instead of saying "Yes". John asked if he could go and change his library book and the teacher nodded her head.

noise

A noise is anything that you can hear. Noise is often unpleasant. Traffic makes a lot of noise in a town.

noisy

Something that is noisy makes a lot of noise. Mr Noisy sneezes so loudly that you can hear him in the next country!

none

None means not any. Mr Greedy has four cakes on his plate but Mr Skinny has none. Mr Skinny's plate is empty.

nonsense

Nonsense is something silly that is said which cannot be true. Mr Nonsense says that dogs wear hats and sheep can fly. What nonsense!

normal

Normal means being like others of the same kind. Tea is normally made with boiling water. But Mr Silly makes his tea with cold lemonade! That's not normal. In fact, it's very unusual.

nose

Your nose sticks out in the middle of your face. You breathe through your nose and use it to smell with.

nosey

A nosey person likes to know all about other people's business. Mr Nosey is always peeping through windows and asking questions. It is hard to keep a secret from him, he is so nosey.

note

A note is a short message that is written down. David's uncle gave him a train set for Christmas, so David wrote him a note to say "Thank you".

A note is also a single sound in music.

notebook

A notebook is a small book to write things in.

notice

A notice is a written warning or message. It is put in a place where everyone can read it. There was a notice by the river saying "No Fishing Allowed".

To notice something is to see it suddenly. Mr Robinson only just noticed Mr Small in time. He nearly trod on him!

nuisance

A nuisance is a person or thing that annoys you. Mandy's younger brother can be a nuisance. He sometimes wants to play his records when she is trying to do her homework.

number

A number is one of a set of symbols or words that you count with. A number tells you how many things there are. For example, 13, 48 and 648 are all numbers.

nurse

A nurse is a person who looks after sick people.

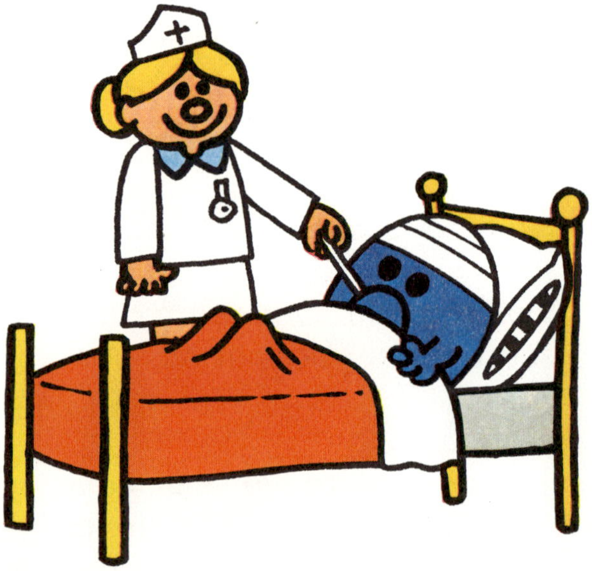

nut

A nut is the dry fruit of some trees. Nuts usually have a hard shell on the outside. You can eat the soft inside of many nuts, such as peanuts and hazelnuts.

oar

An oar is like a long wooden pole with a wide flat end. You row with an oar. Two oars are used to row a rowing boat.

obedient

An obedient person does as he is told.

obey

To obey someone is to do what someone tells you. Sally obeyed her mother and crossed the road at the pedestrian crossing.

object

An object is a thing that you can see and touch. A ball is a round object.

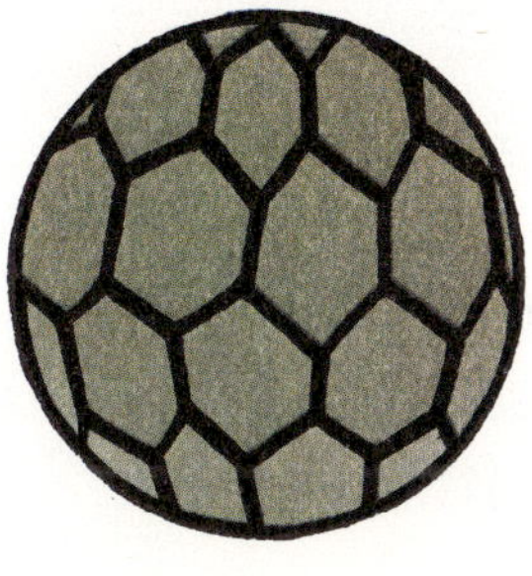

oblong

An oblong is a shape with four sides. Two opposite sides of the shape are longer than the other two. The picture of Mr Skinny is in an oblong frame.

obstacle

An obstacle is something that gets in the way. The bus had to stop because there was an obstacle in its way. The wind had blown a tree down right across the road.

obvious

Something that is obvious is easy to see or understand. There is obviously something wrong with my watch. It keeps stopping.

occasionally

Occasionally means once in a while. Mr Chatterbox occasionally stops talking. But only when he cannot think of anything else to say. And that doesn't happen very often!

occur

To occur is to happen. The accident occurred at lunch time.

When something occurs to you, it means you suddenly think of it. Mr Rush wondered why his tea was cold. Then it occurred to him. He hadn't given the water time to boil first.

ocean

An ocean is a great area of water that surrounds land. An ocean is much bigger than a sea. It can be hundreds of miles across. The Atlantic and Pacific are both oceans.

octopus

An octopus is an animal that lives in the sea. It has eight long arms called tentacles. There are suckers on the arms to help the octopus move along the bottom of the sea.

odd

Odd means strange. Mr Silly's friend invented a very odd car. It had square wheels!

Odd also means not matching or different. Mr Wrong wears odd gloves and odd shoes.

An odd number is not even. If you divide an odd number by two, there will always be one left over. Numbers 3, 7 and 11 are odd numbers.

offer

To offer something is to ask someone if he wants it. Mr Happy offered his guests a drink.

To offer also means to say you are willing to do something. Graham offered to help his mother with the washing up.

office

An office is a room or a building where people work. Office workers usually sit at desks to do their work. Margaret types letters in an office.

often

Often means many times. Mr Lazy often falls asleep in the middle of a television programme.

oil

Oil is a thick greasy liquid. Mineral oil, which comes from under the ground, is used for heating and for making machines run smoothly. Vegetable oil is much thinner and is used for frying food.

To oil is to put oil on something to make it work better. Mr Quiet oiled his lawn mower to stop it squeaking.

old

Old is the opposite of young or new. Old means having existed for a long time. Mr Clever visited an old castle. It had been built hundreds of years ago.

onion

An onion is a vegetable. Onions grow in the ground and are the bulbs of the onion plant. They are round and have a strong taste and smell. You can eat onions raw or cooked.

only

Only means no more than. Mr Skinny eats only one biscuit for his tea.

Only also means one on its own. Adam is the only boy in his class with green eyes.

open

Open means not shut. Mr Fussy left his bedroom window open while he was out, to let some fresh air into the room.

opinion

Your opinion is what you think or believe about something or someone. Mr Clever thought he was The Cleverest Person In The World. That was his opinion of himself. What is your opinion of Mr Clever?

opportunity

An opportunity is a chance to do something. Mr Tickle hoped he would have an opportunity to tickle someone while he was out shopping.

opposite

The opposite means the most different. Hot is the opposite of cold.

Opposite also means on the other side. Mr Quiet is standing opposite Mr Impossible on the tennis court.

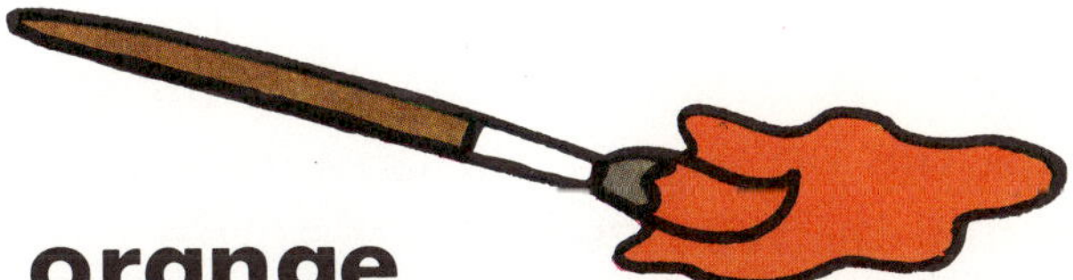

orange

Orange is a colour. It is half-way between red and yellow. Mr Clumsy wears orange shoes.

An orange is also a round, juicy fruit. Oranges grow on trees in hot countries. They have a thick, orange skin that you peel off so that you can eat the soft fruit inside.

orbit

An orbit is the path that one object takes as it moves around another in space. The astronauts came back to earth after their orbit of the moon in a spacecraft.

orchard

An orchard is a piece of land where fruit trees are grown. Apples, pears and cherries are grown in orchards.

orchestra

An orchestra is a large group of people who play musical instruments together. Orchestras usually play music in concert halls or theatres and people pay to hear them.

order

The order is the way that things are arranged. The entries in this dictionary are in alphabetical order.

An order is also something you must obey. Soldiers are trained to obey orders from their officers.

ordinary

Ordinary means usual or common. Mr Happy lives in an ordinary house, but Mr Clever's house is very unusual. In fact, it's very extraordinary!

organise

To organise is to arrange something or put it in order. Mr Brown is organising the school sports this year.

original

Something that is original has not been done or thought of before. Mr Silly thought of an original idea to win the Nonsense Cup. He painted the leaves of a tree green. Nobody had ever seen a tree with green leaves in Nonsenseland before!

original

ornament

An ornament is something that decorates. Mr Clumsy broke one of Mr Uppity's china ornaments when he was dusting.

orphan

An orphan is a child whose parents are dead.

ostrich

ostrich

An ostrich is a bird with a long neck and long legs. Ostriches have wings but they cannot fly. Their long legs help them to run very fast. Ostriches are the largest living birds.

outfit

An outfit is a set of clothes that you wear together. James got a cowboy outfit for his birthday.

outlaw

An outlaw is a person who does not keep to the law. Robin Hood was an outlaw.

outline

The outline of anything is the line that goes right round its outside edge. Mr Clever has drawn an outline of his hand on a piece of paper by going around it with a pencil.

outside

Outside means not inside. Mr Lazy likes to sit outside in the garden on a sunny day, dozing in his deckchair.

oval

Oval means egg-shaped. Mr Forgetful has an oval body but Mr Worry has a round body.

oval

oven

An oven is the part of a cooker where you put food to bake or roast. It is like a heated box with a door.

overalls

You wear overalls over all your other clothes to keep your clothes clean while you are working or playing.

overflow

To overflow is to spill over the top of something because too much has been put in. Mr Forgetful's bath overflowed because he forgot to turn the taps off.

overhear

To overhear is to hear something that you are not meant to hear. Mr Nosey overheard two of his neighbours talking. Mr Nosey couldn't help overhearing them. He had his ear to the wall!

overtake

To overtake means to go past. When a car overtakes another car it goes past it at a faster speed.

owe

To owe is to be in debt and to have to pay back someone for something. Mr Mean owes the library one penny for not returning his books on time.

owl

owl

An owl is a night bird with a large head and eyes. It catches mice and insects to eat. Owls make a hooting sound.

own

Your own is something that is yours and doesn't belong to anyone else. Pat uses her own pen at school. She doesn't need to borrow a school pen.

On your own means being alone. If you are on your own then you are by yourself and there is no one else with you.

pack

To pack is to put things into a box, bag or case. Mr Happy couldn't wait to start packing his suitcase for his holiday at the seaside.

packet

A packet is a small box or an envelope with something sealed inside. Biscuits are sold in packets.

pad

A pad is a lot of sheets of writing or drawing paper stuck together at one edge. Robert wrote down the telephone message on a pad so he wouldn't forget it.

A pad is also a thick piece of material used to make something more comfortable or to stop damage. Cricket players wear pads on their legs to protect them from the ball.

paddle

To paddle is to walk in shallow water. Mr Tall can only paddle at the seaside because the water is not deep enough for him to swim in.

A paddle is a kind of oar. It has a short wooden handle and a flat end for pushing a canoe through water.

page

A page is a sheet of paper in a book or a magazine or a newspaper. Mr Grumpy tears all the pages out of his books instead of reading them. What a bad-tempered fellow!

pain

Pain is an unpleasant feeling. You feel pain when you are hurt. Mr Wrong had a pain in his foot. So he went to see the dentist!

palm

The palm of your hand is the flat part on the inside. Mr Small is so tiny you could hold him in the palm of your hand.

A palm is also a tall tree found in hot places. Dates and coconuts grow on different kinds of palm trees.

palm

paint

Paint is a liquid that is used to colour things. Mr Messy painted his front door with orange paint. But there was more paint on Mr Messy than there was on the door!

pair

A pair is two things that match. Mr Funny bought a new pair of gloves for the winter.

Sometimes a pair is one object that has two matching parts. A pair of trousers has two legs, and a pair of scissors has two blades.

palace

A palace is a large grand building. Kings and queens live in palaces.

pale

Pale means light in colour. People's faces often go pale when they are ill or when they have had a fright.

pan

A pan is a cooking pot. Most pans have a handle and a lid. Frying pans are not very deep and are used to fry food. Saucepans are used on the top of a cooker for boiling and stewing food.

pancake

A pancake is a food made from flour, eggs and milk and cooked in a frying pan. Pancakes are round and thin and about the size of a small dinner plate. People eat pancakes on Pancake Day which is also called Shrove Tuesday.

panda

panda

A panda is an animal that looks like a bear. It lives in China. A panda has white fur, with black patches on its legs, ears and around its eyes.

pandemonium

Pandemonium means a lot of noise and fuss. There was pandemonium in the swimming pool when Mr Mischief let all the water out. The swimmers began to shout and wave their arms about.

panic

To panic is to be suddenly frightened and not know what to do. Mr Jelly panicked when he saw a scarecrow. He thought it was a monster. In a panic, he ran all the way home.

pant

To pant is to breathe in short gasps. You pant when you have been running very fast.

paper

Paper is a thin material that you write on. Paper is made from wood. The pages in this book are made of paper. Paper is also used to wrap parcels and cover walls.

parachute

A parachute is used by people when they have to jump from a flying aeroplane. The parachute enables them to float safely down to the ground. A parachute looks like a large, soft, silky umbrella, with ropes and a harness to hold a person.

The pilot floated safely down to the ground with his parachute.

parcel

A parcel is something that is wrapped in paper and fastened with string or sticky tape. Mr Happy receives lots of parcels at Christmas.

parent

A parent is a father or a mother.

park

A park is a piece of land in a town where people go to enjoy themselves. Most parks have grass and gardens and a children's playground.

To park a car is to leave it in a place by the side of a road or in a car park.

parrot

A parrot is a bird with brightly coloured feathers. Some people keep parrots in cages as pets. Parrots can be taught to talk.

particular

Particular means this one and not any other one. At this particular moment, you are reading the *Mr Men Picture Dictionary.*

particularly

Particularly means especially or very much. Mr Greedy is particularly fond of chocolate biscuits.

partner

partner

A partner is a person who joins with you to do something. Mr Busy chose Mr Rush for his partner in the three-legged race.

party

A party is a time when people come together to enjoy themselves. On her birthday, Tracy had a party for all her friends. They danced to records and played party games.

pass

To pass means to go by or overtake. When he passes a neighbour's house, Mr Nosey always peeps in through the window to see what is going on inside.

To pass something also means to hand something from one person to another. Mr Silly asked Mr Nonsense to pass him another cup of cold porridge.

passage

A passage is a narrow path or tunnel or alleyway. The smugglers escaped through a secret passage in the wall of the cottage.

passage

passenger

A passenger is a person who travels in a vehicle that someone else is driving. There are six passengers on this bus.

past

The past is time that is over or finished. In the past, there were no cars or aeroplanes.

Past means beyond a place or time. Mr Uppity walked right past Mr Happy without saying "Hello". How rude of him!

paste

Paste is a thick mixture used to stick things together.

pastry

Pastry is a mixture of flour, fat and water. You roll it out with a rolling pin. Pastry is used to make pies and sausage rolls. It is baked in a hot oven.

patch

A patch is a small area. There was a damp patch on the carpet after Mr Clumsy had spilt a glass of water.

A patch is also a small piece of material used to cover a hole in a pair of trousers or a jacket or a worn sleeve.

path

A path is a narrow track where people can walk through the woods or in a garden or by a river. A path is much narrower than a road. Cars are not allowed on a path.

patient

A patient person is content to wait calmly for something and doesn't complain. Mr Slow is very patient. He waited two hours for the bus to arrive. Two hours! And he didn't mind a bit.

A patient is also a sick person who is being looked after by doctors and nurses.

pattern

A pattern is made up of colours, shapes and lines arranged in a particular way. Wallpaper and dress materials are often decorated with patterns.

pavement

A pavement is the pathway along the side of a road. People walk on the pavement but cars are not allowed to drive there. The pavement is usually made from hard material like concrete.

paw

A paw is the foot of an animal with claws.

pay

To pay is to give money for something that is being bought or for work done. Mr Topsy Turvy paid the taxi driver for driving him to his hotel.

pea

A pea is a vegetable. Peas are the round, green seeds of a plant. They grow with others inside a pod.

peace

Peace is a time when there is no war.

Peace also means quietness and stillness. Mr Quiet likes to live in the peace of the countryside. It is so peaceful, away from the noise of the traffic in the town.

peach

A peach is a soft, juicy fruit with a furry skin. Peaches grow on trees in hot countries.

pear

A pear is a green or yellow fruit that grows on a tree. It is shaped like a bell.

pebble

A pebble is a small round smooth stone. At the seaside some beaches are covered with pebbles instead of sand.

peculiar

Peculiar means strange or unusual. Mr Funny lives in a peculiar place. He lives in a teapot!

pedal

A pedal is a part of a machine that is worked by foot. When you ride a bicycle, you put your feet on two pedals to push the wheels round. A driver pushes the pedals on a car to make it go faster or stop.

peel

To peel is to take the outer skin off a fruit or vegetable.

peep

To peep is to take a quick look at something. Mr Nosey peeped through a gap in the fence to see what was on the other side.

pen

You use a pen to write with. Pens have a writing tip or nib and are filled with ink. There are felt-tip pens, fountain pens and ballpoint pens.

A pen is also a place to keep sheep for a short time.

pencil

A pencil is used for writing and drawing. It has a dark grey lead in the middle. You need a sharp pencil to draw a thin line.

penguin

penguin

A penguin is a bird that cannot fly. Penguins have white fronts, with black feathers on their backs and tails. They use their wings for swimming and have webbed feet. Penguins live near the South Pole.

people

People means a number of men, women or children. There were a lot of people on the beach because it was such a hot day.

pepper

Pepper is a powder that you put on food to give it flavour. Pepper has a hot taste. Pepper can be black, white or red.

perfect

Something that is perfect has nothing wrong with it at all. Mr Fussy was very proud of his perfect lawn. Every blade of grass was neatly cut and perfectly straight.

perform

To perform is to entertain people in a theatre or a hall. The school performed a play at the end of term.

perform

perhaps

Perhaps means maybe. Perhaps it will rain tomorrow.

permanent

Something that is permanent is always there and it lasts for a long time. Mr Bump has a permanent bruise on his head, because he is always walking into things!

permission

Permission is being allowed to do something. The headmaster gave the children permission to play games on the last day of term.

permit

To permit is to allow someone to do something. You are permitted to fish in this river if you ask first.

permit

perplexed

Perplexed means puzzled or confused. Mr Clever was quite perplexed when Mr Small asked him how he could grow bigger. Mr Clever didn't know the answer.

person

A person is a man or woman or child.

persuade

To persuade means to make someone do something by making him think that it is the best thing to do. Mr Happy persuaded Mr Mean to have his roof mended. Mr Mean finally agreed, because he was tired of getting wet every time it rained.

pest

A pest is someone or something that is a nuisance. Greenfly are a pest to gardeners, because they kill the flowers.

pet

pet

A pet is an animal that you keep in the house. Many people keep dogs or cats as pets.

petal

A petal is one of the coloured parts of a flower. Daffodils have yellow petals.

petrol

Petrol is a liquid fuel that comes from oil. It is used to make many sorts of engines work. Cars and motorbikes use petrol.

photograph

A photograph is a picture taken with a camera. You can take photographs of all sorts of things like people or places or animals.

piano

A piano is a large musical instrument. It has a row of white and black keys. When you press the keys down, each one makes a different sound.

piano

pick

To pick is to choose. Mr Mean always picks the cheapest things in the supermarket when he goes shopping.

To pick also means to gather something that is growing. In the autumn you can pick blackberries from bushes.

To pick up means to lift. Mr Strong picked up a heavy stone with no effort at all.

picnic

A picnic is a meal that you eat outside on an outing. Mr Clumsy and Mr Muddle had a picnic at the seaside. Mr Clumsy dropped one of his sandwiches in the sand!

picture

A picture is a drawing or a painting or a photograph. Mr Messy likes painting pictures. But he always manages to get the paint all over the floor as well as the picture!

pie

A pie is made of pastry filled with fruit or meat or some other kind of food. Pies are cooked in an oven and can be eaten hot or cold.

piece

A piece is a part that has been broken off or cut away from something. Mr Quiet found a piece of driftwood on the beach.

pig

A pig is an animal that lives on a farm. It has a flat snout for a nose and a short curly tail. Pork, ham and bacon come from pigs.

pile

A pile is a heap of things, one on top of the other. Mr Messy always has several piles of dirty dishes in his kitchen, waiting to be washed.

pill

A pill is a solid type of medicine. The doctor gives you pills to swallow when you are ill.

pillarbox

A pillarbox is for posting letters. There is a wide opening near the top to put the letters in. Most pillarboxes are in the street and postmen come several times a day to empty them.

pillow

A pillow is a soft pad that you rest your head on in bed. It is made from a cloth bag filled with something soft and light like feathers or foam.

pilot

A pilot is a person who flies an aeroplane.

pin

A pin is a small thin piece of metal. It has a sharp point at one end and a round head at the other. Pins are used to hold pieces of material or paper together.

pinch

To pinch is to nip or squeeze something between your finger and thumb. David cried when his sister pinched his arm.

pink

Pink is a colour. If you mix red and white paint together you will make pink. Mr Lazy is pink.

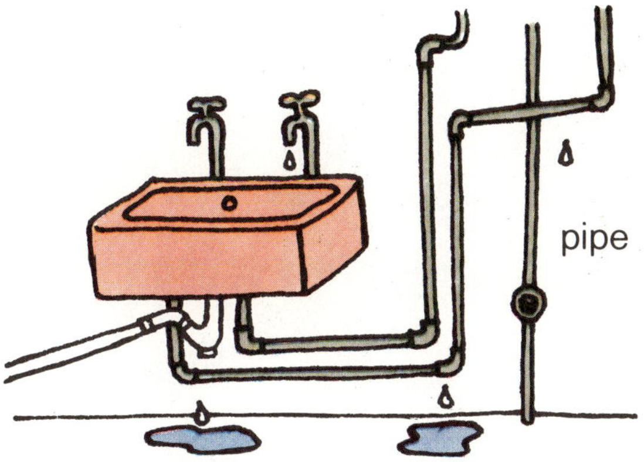

pipe

A pipe is a long hollow tube made of metal, plastic or rubber. Water goes along pipes to reach the taps in your kitchen and bathroom.

plain

Plain means ordinary. Mr Greedy doesn't like plain cakes. He likes cakes covered with icing or chocolate.

Plain also means clear. The passengers in the aeroplane could plainly see the fields and houses on the ground below.

plan

To plan is to decide how you are going to do something before you start. Mr Clever planned his camping holiday very carefully. He decided where he was going to stay, and made a list of everything he would need.

planet

A planet is one of the very large round bodies that move around the sun. The earth is a planet. So are Mars and Venus.

plank

A plank is a flat length of wood. Mr Muddle is trying to build a shed from planks of wood. What a muddle!

plant

A plant is anything that grows in the ground. Trees and flowers are plants.

To plant is to put a seed or a small plant in the ground so that it will grow. Mr Fussy plants all his flowers in neat little rows.

plastic

Plastic is a man-made material that is used for making many things. Cups and plates that are made of plastic do not easily break. Can you see any plastic things around you?

plate

A plate is a flat dish that you put food on. Most plates are round.

platform

A platform is like a small stage at one end of a room or hall. Sally went up on to the platform to receive her swimming medal.

A platform is also a part of a railway station. It is higher than the railway track. You stand on the platform to wait for the train.

play

To play is to do something that is fun. The children played happily in the garden until it was time to go to bed.

To play also means to take part in a game. Do you know how to play chess?

A play is a story that is acted on a stage, on the radio or on television.

please

To please is to make someone happy. Mr Chatterbox is always pleased to have someone to talk to.

Please is a polite word to say when you ask for something. "Pass me that pencil, please," said Mr Small.

plenty

Plenty means a lot of or as much as is needed. Mr Funny knows plenty of jokes. He never tells the same one twice.

plug

A plug is a round piece of rubber, plastic or wood used to block up a hole. Most sinks have a plug to stop the water running down the drain.

An electrical plug connects a machine to an electricity supply. A television works when it is plugged in and switched on.

plum

A plum is a soft round fruit. It has a large stone in the middle. Plums grow on trees. Ripe plums are red, purple or yellow.

pocket

A pocket is like a small bag inside a coat or a pair of trousers. You can keep small things like a handkerchief or money in your pocket.

point

A point is the sharp end of something. Pins, needles and sharp pencils have points.

To point is to show with a finger. Mr Dizzy pointed to a word in his book that he did not know. Mr Clever told him what it was.

poison

Poison will kill you or make you very ill if you eat or drink it. Some kinds of berries are poisonous.

poke

To poke is to jab something sharply with a stick or finger. Andy poked his friend in the back and asked if he could borrow his pencil sharpener.

policeman

A policeman helps and protects people and stops others from breaking the law. When Mr Muddle lost his way in the town, a friendly policeman helped him.

policeman

polish

To polish something is to rub it until it shines. Mr Fussy polishes all his cups and plates every time he washes them.

polite

A polite person has good manners and is not rude. It is polite to say "Please" and "Thank you".

pollution

Pollution is spoiling the air, sea and land with unpleasant things like rubbish, fumes and leaking oil. The fumes from car engines pollute the air we breathe.

pond

A pond is a small hollow filled with water. Some people have a pond in their garden, with goldfish in it. Ponds are smaller than lakes.

pond

ponder

To ponder is to think about something carefully for a time. The doctor pondered over Mr Bounce's problem. How was he to stop him bouncing all over the place? Then he came up with the answer. Mr Bounce must wear a pair of heavy boots!

pool

A pool is an area of liquid. Swimming pools are specially built for people to swim in. After the rain, there were pools of water on the lawn.

poor

Poor means having little money. Mr Mean pretends to be poor. But he isn't really. He has lots of money hidden away.

Poor also means unlucky or suffering. Poor Mr Quiet couldn't get to sleep because the wind was rustling the leaves of the trees around his house.

Poor also means not very good. Mr Clumsy is poor at games. He keeps dropping the ball!

popular

Popular means liked by many people. Playing and watching football is a popular hobby.

porridge

Porridge is a breakfast food made from oats. Mr Nonsense eats porridge on toast!

portrait

A portrait is a picture of a person. Here is a portrait of Mr Sneeze.

position

The position of something is how or where it is. Mr Bump fell head first into a hole. He stayed in that position until someone pulled him out.

possessions

Your possessions are the things that you own. Mr Strong packed up all his possessions into two large trunks when he moved house.

possible

Possible means able to happen. It is possible to stand on your hands. But it is not possible to stand on no hands. Unless you are Mr Impossible!

post

A post is an upright piece of wood, metal or concrete fixed into the ground. Posts are used to hold up a fence or a gate.

To post is to send a letter by sticking a stamp on it and putting it in a pillarbox.

poster

A poster is a large notice or picture stuck on a wall. Mr Funny saw a poster in the window of the sweetshop. It said that there was a circus coming to town.

potato

A potato is a vegetable. Potatoes grow in the ground at the root of the plant. They have brown skins that you can peel off before cooking them.

pour

To pour is to make liquid flow from one place to another. Mr Wrong poured out a cup of tea. And missed! Most of it went in the saucer, the rest went on the floor.

To pour also means to rain heavily.

powder

Powder is like very fine dust. It is made by crushing or grinding something. Flour is a powder made by crushing grains of wheat or corn.

power

Power is force or strength. Electricity provides power to make machines work.

practically

Practically means almost. Mr Busy and Mr Slow had dinner together. Mr Busy had practically finished his meal before Mr Slow had eaten his first mouthful!

practise

To practise is to do something over and over again until you can do it well. Tina practised her recorder every day.

pram

A pram is like a cot on wheels that is used to take a baby for a walk.

pram

prayer

A prayer is what you say when you speak to God. We say prayers in our school assembly.

precious

Precious means worth a lot. Gold is a precious metal.

precisely

Precisely means exactly. According to Mr Tall's clock, it is precisely five o'clock.

precisely

prefer

To prefer is to like one thing better than something else. Mr Greedy is quite fond of fruit cake. But he prefers chocolate cake with lots of cream and icing!

prepare

To prepare is to get something ready. Mr Happy prepared his dinner before he went out. He peeled the potatoes and chopped up the carrots. Then he was able to start cooking his meal as soon as he came in.

present

present

A present is something you give to someone else. Presents are often wrapped up in pretty paper. People give you presents on your birthday and at Christmas.

press

To press is to push on something. Mr Mischief pressed Mr Uppity's front doorbell. Then he ran away!

pretend

To pretend is to make believe something that is not real or true. Mr Skinny dressed up in a sheet and pretended to be a ghost. But he didn't frighten anybody!

pretend

pretty

Pretty means nice to look at. Alison looked very pretty in her new party dress.

price

The price of something is how much it costs. Mr Grumpy grumbled about the price of cornflakes. He said it was much too high.

prick

To prick is to make a small hole with a sharp point. Mr Clumsy pricked his finger with a needle when he was trying to sew a button on his shirt.

prince

A prince is the son of a king or queen.

princess

A princess is the daughter of a king or queen.

princess prince

print

To print is to put letters, words or pictures on paper using a machine or a special tool.
A newspaper is printed on a machine called a printing press. This can print hundreds of copies very quickly.

prison

A prison is a place where someone is locked away. People who have broken the law are sent to prison. A prison is also called a jail.

private

Something that is private is meant to be used or seen by the person to whom it belongs. It is not for everybody. If a door or gate is marked "Private" it means that you should not go in without the owner's permission.

procession

prize

A prize is something that you win in a competition or a game. Mr Rush won a prize for winning the running race. The prize was a big silver cup.

probably

Probably means very likely or almost certainly. Mr Forgetful will probably forget something next time he goes shopping.

problem

A problem is a very difficult question or situation. Mr Bounce wondered how he could solve his problem of bouncing all over the place.

procession

A procession is a large number of people or vehicles moving together in a long line. When the circus came to town, brass bands, clowns and acrobats marched along in the procession.

produce

To produce is to make something. The factory at the end of our road produces tinned food.

To produce also means to bring out. The magician produced a rabbit from a hat.

programme

A programme is something that is shown on television or heard on the radio.

A programme is also a list of people in a play, or of the music being played or sung in a concert.

promise

To promise is to give your word that you will do something. People are expected to keep their promises and not break them. Philip promised his mother he would be home by six o'clock.

proof

Proof is something that shows that a fact is true. The treacle in Mr Funny's hat was proof that Mr Mischief had been up to his tricks again.

proper

Proper means right or the most suitable. Mr Noisy didn't have a proper hammer. So he used one of his heavy shoes to hammer a nail into the wall!

protect

To protect something means to keep it from harm. Mr Jelly built a high wall round his house to protect it from burglars.

proud

proud

When you are proud of something you are very pleased with it. Mr Clever is very proud of his new invention. It is a machine that not only washes and dries clothes, but also irons them and puts them away!

prove

To prove is to show that something is true. You can prove that the Mr Men are in this book by looking at them yourself!

provide

To provide means to give something that is needed. Cows provide us with milk and sheep provide us with wool.

prune

A prune is a dried plum. It is a dark brown fruit with a wrinkled skin. There is a large stone in the middle.

To prune is to cut off branches from a tree, bush or hedge.

pry

To pry is to be nosey. Mr Nosey is always prying into other people's affairs by asking questions and looking through keyholes.

pudding

A pudding is something sweet that you eat after the main part of a meal. Puddings can be hot or cold.

puddle

A puddle is a small pool of water. There were puddles of water in the road after the heavy rain.

pull

To pull is to try to move something towards you. Mr Muddle pulled on the handle of the shop door as hard as he could, but the door wouldn't open. So he pushed it instead, and the door opened at once!

pump

A pump is a machine used to force liquid or gas into something. A bicycle pump is used to fill a bicycle tyre with air.

punch

To punch is to hit someone or something with your fist.

punish

To punish someone is to make him suffer because he has done something wrong. The giant punished Mr Greedy for being greedy, by making him eat the most enormous meal he had ever seen. Mr Greedy felt very ill afterwards.

puppet

A puppet is a small doll or toy animal that can be made to move. Some puppets are worked by strings attached to their legs and arms. Glove puppets fit over your hand and you move your fingers to make them work.

purple

Purple is a colour. It is between blue and red.

purse

A purse is a small bag that is used to hold money. Most purses fasten with a clip or a zip to keep the money inside.

push

To push is to press hard on something to make it move away from you. When Mr Funny's car broke down, Mr Strong pushed it all the way home.

puzzle

A puzzle is something that is difficult to do or solve. Mr Dizzy spent all week trying to do a crossword puzzle. By the end of the week he'd only solved one clue. And that was wrong!

pyramid

A pyramid is a shape that has a square bottom and four sides shaped like triangles. The triangles meet in a point at the top. In ancient Egypt huge pyramids of stone were built in honour of past kings and queens.

quarrel

To quarrel is to argue and to disagree. The children quarrelled about who should ride the bicycle first.

quarter

If you divide something into four equal parts, each part will be a quarter.

queen

A queen is a woman who rules a country or is the wife of a king.

question

A question is something that you ask to find out something. When you ask a question, you expect to be given an answer.

queue

A queue is a line of people waiting for something. There is a long queue of people outside the cinema.

queue

quick

Quick means fast or taking only a very short time. Mr Busy does everything very quickly. It only takes him half a minute to mow his lawn.

quick

quiet

Something that is quiet makes hardly any noise. Mr Quiet does not have a loud voice. He talks so quietly that nobody can hear him!

quite

Quite means completely. It is quite clear that we cannot finish this work today.

Quite also means rather. Mr Bounce is quite small. He is about as big as a tennis ball. But Mr Small is very small indeed. He is about as small as a marble!

quite

quiver

To quiver is to shake and tremble. Mr Jelly quivers when he is frightened. Just like a jelly quivers when you shake it!

quiver

quiz

A quiz is a game in which teams or people try to answer the most questions correctly. Sometimes we have a spelling quiz at school.

rabbit

A rabbit is a small animal with long ears and a short fluffy tail. Rabbits live in burrows underground. Pet rabbits are kept in hutches.

race

A race is a competition to see who can complete a course in the fastest time. There are running, swimming and obstacle races. People drive cars and ride horses in races, too.

radiator

A radiator gives out heat to warm a room. Hot water or steam runs through metal pipes to keep the radiator warm.

radio

A radio receives sounds that come through the air without using wires. You can listen to music and to people talking on the radio.

rag

A rag is a piece of torn or worn out cloth. People use rags for cleaning things. A puppy likes to tear things into rags!

railway

A railway is the track that trains run on. A railway also includes all the trains, stations, level crossings, signals and people that work on the railway.

rain

Rain is the drops of water that fall from clouds in the sky. Mr Muddle got very wet when he went for a walk in the rain.

rainbow

A rainbow is a curve of coloured light in the sky. You see a rainbow when it is raining and the sun is shining at the same time. There are seven colours in a rainbow. They are red, orange, yellow, green, blue, indigo and violet.

raise

To raise something means to lift it up. Jack raised his hand to show that he knew the answer to the teacher's question.

rake

A rake is a garden tool with a long handle. It has a row of spikes which look like teeth at one end. A rake is used to gather leaves or grass and to make the soil smooth and even.

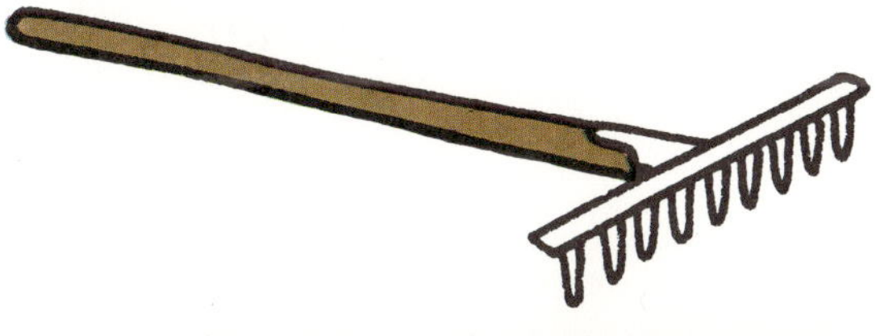

rapid

Rapid means very quick. When Mr Mischief has been up to one of his tricks, he rapidly runs away so that he will not get caught.

rare

Rare means not often seen or found. A four-leaved clover is rare. You will be lucky if you find one.

rash

A rash is a large number of tiny red spots on your skin. A rash can itch.

raspberry

A raspberry is a small, soft red fruit with lots of pips. Raspberries grow on bushes. You can use them to make jam.

rather

Rather means quite. Mr Mischief gave Mr Chatterbox a rather unusual hat. It was filled with raspberry jam!

Rather also means liking something better. Mr Lazy would rather sleep all day than go for a walk.

rattle

To rattle is to make a series of short, sharp sounds. The wind made the doors and windows of Mr Jelly's house rattle. Mr Jelly was very frightened. He thought the house would fall down.

A rattle is a baby's toy that makes a noise when it is shaken.

raw

Raw means not cooked. Carrots can be eaten raw or cooked.

reach

To reach means to get to. It took Mr Topsy Turvy an hour to reach the station. He was slow getting there because he walked backwards all the way!

To reach also means to stretch out and touch. Mr Tickle can reach round corners with his extraordinarily long arms. He reached through the classroom window and tickled the teacher.

read

To read is to look at and understand words that are written down. Mr Clever has read every book in the library. Twice!

To read also means to say out loud something that is written down.

ready

Ready means able to start. Mr Busy called for Mr Slow to go to the cinema. But Mr Slow wasn't ready.

real

Real means true and not false. Paper flowers are not real but the flowers growing in the garden are real.

realise

To realise means to understand eventually. Mr Dizzy wondered why his living room seemed darker than usual. After a while, he realised he had forgotten to draw back the curtains!

reason

The reason for something is why it happens. The reason why Mr Bump is always wearing bandages is that he keeps hurting himself.

receive

To receive is to be given something. Mr Quiet received an invitation to Mr Happy's party. The postman gave it to him.

recipe

A recipe tells you how to cook something. A cake recipe tells you what food you need to make the cake, how to mix it, and how long to cook it for.

recognise

To recognise is to know someone or something you have seen before. Mr Slow recognised his old friend as soon as he saw him. He recognised him even though he hadn't seen him for many years.

record

You play a record on a record player and it produces music.

A record is also the very best known performance of something. Mr Rush broke the world record for delivering letters. He delivered 60 letters to 60 people in one minute! What a record!

recover

To recover means to get better after an illness or a shock. Susan was not allowed to go swimming until she had recovered from flu.

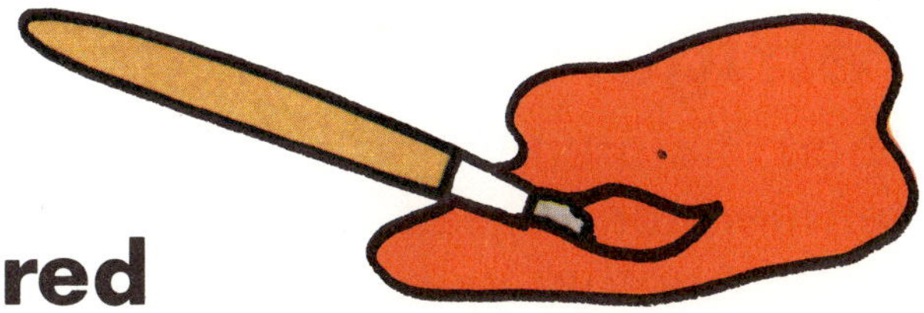

red

Red is the colour of a ripe tomato. Mr Muddle wears a red hat.

reduce

To reduce is to make smaller or less. Mr Chatterbox bought a new hat in a sale at a reduced price. It was reduced to half price.

reflect

A shiny surface, like a mirror, reflects an object that is put in front of it. It shows an exact picture of the object. These trees are reflected in the water.

reflect

reflection

A reflection is what you see in a mirror or a shiny surface. When you comb your hair, it helps to look at your reflection in a mirror to see what you are doing.

refrigerator

Food is stored inside a refrigerator to keep it cool and fresh. Another word for a refrigerator is a fridge.

refuse

To refuse is to say no to something or not allow it. Mr Grumpy refused to let his neighbour borrow his lawn mower.

register

A register is a list of names. A school register contains the names and addresses of all the children in a class. Every day the teacher marks the register to show how many children are at school and how many are away.

register

regret

To regret is to be sorry or to wish that something had not happened. Mr Dizzy regretted leaving the gate open. All the sheep got out into the lane. The farmer was cross!

rehearsal

To have a rehearsal is to practise. Actors usually have several rehearsals before they perform a play in front of an audience.

relation

Your relations are the people who belong to your family. Your uncles and aunts are your relations. So are your grandparents and cousins.

relax

To relax is to rest and let your body feel at ease. Mr Lazy likes to relax in a deckchair. All day!

release

To release something means to let it go free. The boy released the bird that was trapped inside the room. He opened the window and let it fly away.

relief

Relief is a feeling of pleasure that something bad is over or is not going to happen. It was a relief for Mr Jelly to wake up from his terrible dream.

rely

To rely on means to depend on someone. When someone tells you a secret they rely on you not to tell anyone else.

remarkable

Remarkable means unusual and worth noticing. Mr Impossible can do some remarkable things, such as walking up the side of a tree!

remarkable

remember

To remember is to keep something in your mind and not forget it.

remind

To remind is to help someone remember something. Mr Forgetful left his toothbrush on the table to remind himself to go to the dentist.

remove

To remove is to take away or take off. You remove your clothes when you have a bath.

repair

repair

To repair is to mend something and make it useful again. Mr Fussy had to repair his garden gate after Mr Clumsy had broken the handle.

repeat

To repeat is to say or do something again. Mr Quiet often has to repeat what he has said because people cannot hear him the first time.

replace

To replace is to put something back where it belongs. You must replace the lid on the biscuit tin to keep the biscuits fresh.

To replace also means to put one thing in place of another. Mr Mischief stole the wizard's magic wand and replaced it with a broomstick.

reply

To reply is to answer either by speaking or writing. When Mr Tall received an invitation to a party he replied straight away. He wrote to say he would love to go.

report

A report is a description of something that has happened or has been done. Your teacher writes a report about your work.

reptile

A reptile is a cold-blooded animal. Its body is covered with scales. Some reptiles have very short legs and others have no legs at all. Snakes, lizards, crocodiles and tortoises are all reptiles.

request

A request is something that has been asked for. Disc jockeys receive requests to play records on their programmes.

rescue

To rescue is to save someone from harm or danger. A lifeboat came to rescue Mr Bump when he fell off a boat into the sea.

respect

To respect is to admire someone and behave well towards him. The crew of the fishing boat had a great respect for their captain.

responsible

Responsible means taking care of something. A bus driver is responsible for the safety of his passengers.

Responsible also means having made something happen. The teacher demanded to know who was responsible for breaking the window.

rest

To rest is to sit or lie down and be still for a while. Mr Busy never has time to rest. He always finds another little job to do.

The rest means what is left over. Mr Skinny ate a few crumbs of his doughnut and gave the rest to Mr Greedy.

restaurant

A restaurant is a place where you pay to eat a meal. Mr Uppity often eats in a restaurant.

result

The result is what happens because of something else. Mr Strong is very strong as a result of eating lots of eggs.

A result is also the final score or mark in a test or a competition.

return

To return is to go back to where you came from. When Mr Greedy goes shopping he always returns with an overflowing basket.

To return also means to give back. If you borrow a pencil you should return it as soon as you have finished using it.

reveal

To reveal is to show something that has been hidden. Mr Robinson picked up a leaf and revealed Mr Small hiding under it.

revenge

Revenge is paying someone back for a wrong thing that has been done to you. The clever pig and the clever elephant made fun of Mr Dizzy and upset him. But later that day, Mr Dizzy got his revenge by playing tricks on them and making them look silly.

reward

A reward is given in return for help or bravery. The boy received a reward for finding the lost dog.

rhyme

Words that rhyme sound like each other. "Cat" rhymes with "hat". "Dog" rhymes with "fog".

A rhyme is a verse that has rhyming words at the end of each line. Can you think of a rhyme?

ribbon

A ribbon is a long, narrow piece of coloured material. A ribbon is used to keep things together. You can tie your hair with ribbons.

rice

Rice is a plant that produces grain that we eat. Rice comes from hot countries and grows in fields of water called paddy fields. Rice is cooked before it is eaten.

rich

Rich means having a lot of money or goods.

rid

To get rid of means to be free of something by throwing it away or destroying it. Mr Clever invented a new kind of mousetrap to get rid of the mice in his shed.

ride

To ride is to travel on an animal or in a vehicle. Many people ride in cars and some people ride on horses. Which would you prefer?

ridiculous

ridiculous

Ridiculous means really silly. In Nonsenseland people do ridiculous things like putting wallpaper on the outside of their houses!

right

Right means correct and not wrong. Joe had full marks in the test because he got all the answers right.

Right also means on the opposite side to the left. Mr Noisy holds his pencil in his right hand when he is drawing.

right

ring

A ring is a circle with a space in the middle. People wear rings on their fingers.

To ring is to make the sound of a bell. The church bells ring every Sunday morning. The telephone rings when you have dialled somebody's number.

ripe

Ripe means fully grown and ready for eating. Most fruits change colour as they become ripe. A tomato is red when it is ripe.

rise

To rise means to go up. The smoke from a fire rises up the chimney.

To rise also means to get up from lying down, sitting or kneeling. Mr Tall stretches his long legs when he rises from bed in the morning.

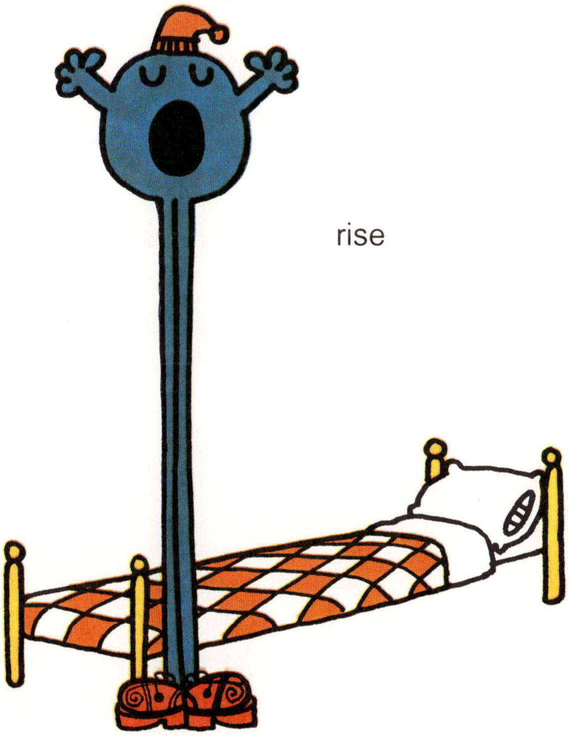

rise

risk

A risk is a chance of danger or misfortune. Racing drivers take risks when they drive their cars very fast. If you go out without a raincoat when it looks like rain, you will have to risk getting wet.

river

A river is like a large moving stream. Rivers flow from high ground down to the sea or a lake.

river

road

A road is a wide hard track that goes from one place to another. Roads are built for cars and other vehicles to travel on.

roar

To roar is to make a loud, deep, harsh sound. Thunder roars and so does a lion. The lion at the zoo roared at Mr Jelly and gave him a terrible fright.

To roar with laughter is to laugh very loudly.

roast

To roast is to cook food in an oven or over a fire. We had roast meat for Sunday lunch.

rob

To rob is to steal something from another person. There was a robbery at the bank last week. The thieves robbed the safe and took all the money.

rock

A rock is a large lump of stone. Mr Strong is so strong, he can pick up a rock in one hand and balance it on his head!

Rock is also a hard sweet. At the seaside you can buy a long stick of rock.

To rock is to move gently from side to side or backwards and forwards. Mr Lazy likes to rock back and forth in his rocking chair.

rocket

A rocket is a firework that shoots up into the air very quickly.

A rocket is also a type of space vehicle. Big rockets are used to send men into space.

roll

To roll is to move along by turning over and over. A ball rolls easily because it is round. So do wheels.

A roll also means something round. A bread roll is a small round lump of bread.

roof

A roof is the top covering of a building. Most houses have a sloping roof, so that the rain can run off into the gutters at the sides. A roof is usually covered with tiles.

room

A room is part of the inside of a house or building. A room has four walls, a floor and a ceiling. The rooms in Mr Funny's house are an odd shape because he lives in a teapot. His house has five rooms. There are two bedrooms, a bathroom, a kitchen and a living room.

root

The root is the part of a plant that grows under the ground. The roots of a plant hold it firm in the ground and take in food from the soil. Carrots are the roots of the carrot plant.

root

rope

rope

A rope is strong, thick string. Rope is used for tying up or pulling heavy objects. You can pull a car that has broken down with a rope. A rope is also used for skipping.

rose

A rose is a sweet-smelling flower with a prickly stem. Roses grow on bushes in gardens or on hedges in the countryside. Roses can be many different colours such as red, pink, yellow, white or orange.

rot

To rot is to go bad. Food rots if it is left around for a long time. Mr Greedy's food never has time to go rotten. He eats it as soon as he has bought it!

rough

Rough means not smooth. Sandpaper feels rough if you rub your finger over it.

Rough also means not gentle. Boys are rough when they fight each other.

A rough sea has lots of waves. The sea is very rough during a storm.

round

Round means shaped like a circle or a ball. Mr Happy, Mr Bounce and Mr Small all have round bodies.

round

row

A row is a line of things or people. Seats in a cinema are arranged in rows.

To row is to push a boat along with oars.

royal

Royal means to do with kings and queens. The King of the Goblins is a royal person.

rub

To rub is to wipe hard with something and move it backwards and forwards over a surface. Mr Fussy rubbed Mr Messy's dirty fingermarks off the door with a damp cloth.

rubber

Rubber comes from the sap of the rubber tree. Car tyres are made of rubber. So are wellington boots. Mr Bounce bounces like a rubber ball.

A rubber is also a small piece of rubber or plastic used to rub out pencil marks on paper.

rubbish

Rubbish is all the things that are useless or worn out or not wanted. People usually put their rubbish in a dustbin.

Rubbish also means nonsense. Mr Nonsense talks a lot of rubbish. He says that sleeping in a rowing boat is more comfortable than sleeping in a motor boat. What nonsense!

rude

Rude means bad-mannered and not polite. Mr Uppity is often rude. Instead of saying "Excuse me", he pushes people rudely out of the way.

rug

A rug is a small mat used to cover part of a floor. The cat curled up on a rug in front of the fire.

ruin

To ruin is to spoil something so it is no use at all. Mr Forgetful's cakes were ruined because he forgot to take them out of the oven. They were all burnt.

A ruin is what is left of an old building. In some parts of the country you can see the ruins of castles that were built hundreds of years ago.

rule

A rule tells you what you are supposed to do. When you play a game of chess you have to follow the rules.

To rule also means to be at the head of a country. The king ruled for twenty years.

ruler

A ruler is a length of wood, metal or plastic that is used for measuring and drawing straight lines. Mr Clever used a ruler to draw an exact picture of his house.

run

To run is to move quickly on foot. Running is faster than walking. Mr Busy runs everywhere.

rush

To rush is to go fast or do things too quickly. Mr Rush never has time to finish anything, because he is always rushing off to do something else.

rust

Rust is a red coating that forms on metals like iron or steel when they have been allowed to stay wet for some time. If you leave your bike out in the rain it may go rusty.

sack

A sack is a large bag made of thick, strong material. You can carry heavy things like potatoes and coal in sacks. Mr Snow helped Father Christmas with his huge sack of toys.

sad

Sad means unhappy. When you are sad you don't feel like smiling or laughing. People often cry when they are sad.

saddle

A saddle is a leather seat. You sit in a saddle when you ride a horse. A saddle is also the part of a bicycle that you sit on.

The cowboy put a saddle on his horse.

safe

Safe means out of danger or free from harm. A harbour is a safe place for boats.

sail

A sail is a large area of strong cloth fixed to a mast in the middle of a boat. The wind blows into the sail and pushes the boat along.

salad

A salad is a mixture of vegetables such as lettuce, tomatoes and cucumber that you eat cold.

A fruit salad is a mixture of different kinds of fruit such as oranges, pears and grapes.

salt

Salt is like fine white sand. Salt comes from sea-water or from underground mines. We sprinkle salt on to our food to make it tasty.

same

The same means exactly alike and not different. Mr Noisy's shoes are both the same colour. But Mr Wrong's are quite different. One is brown and the other is black.

sand

Sand is made up of tiny grains of crushed rocks. There are miles of sandy beaches at the seaside, where you can build sandcastles.

sandwich

A sandwich is two slices of buttered bread with a tasty filling inbetween. Mr Strong loves sandwiches filled with eggs, eggs and eggs!

sandwich

satisfy

To satisfy means to be good enough. Martin's teacher was satisfied with his work, so she gave him a star.

sauce

Sauce is a thick liquid that you eat with food to make it more tasty. Mr Nonsense puts tomato sauce on his apple pie! Ugh!

saucer

A saucer is a small, shallow dish that is put under a cup. It catches any drips that spill out of the cup.

sausage

A sausage is a roll of minced meat inside a thin skin case. Mr Wrong wore a string of sausages around his neck. He never does anything right!

sausage

save

To save is to take out of danger. The lifeboat men pulled the children out of the sea and saved them from drowning.

To save also means to keep something. Michael saves half his pocket money every week. When he has saved enough money, he will buy a new football.

scatter

To scatter means to throw or drop small pieces of something all over the place. Mr Clumsy scattered cornflakes on the floor.

school

School is a place where children go to learn.

saw

A saw is a tool used for cutting wood and metal. It has a metal blade with sharp teeth along one edge. Wood cutters use a saw to cut trees into logs.

scare

To scare means to frighten. Mr Jelly was very scared when he saw a cat in the garden. He thought it was a ferocious lion.

scarf

You wear a scarf around your neck or your head to keep you warm. Mr Snow wears a woollen scarf with red and white stripes.

scissors

A pair of scissors has two sharp blades fixed together. Scissors are used for cutting paper and cloth and many other things.

score

The score is the number of points or goals made by each team or player in a game. The score at the end of the netball match was six all. Both teams had scored six goals.

scrap

A scrap is a small piece of something. Sally wrote down Sue's telephone number on a scrap of paper.

scratch

To scratch something is to make a mark on it with a sharp or pointed object. Mr Bump scratched the paint on the tractor when he drove too close to the gatepost.

To scratch also means to rub something that itches.

scream

To scream is to make a very loud noise because you are frightened or in pain. Janet screamed when she thought she saw a ghost in her bedroom. But it was only her brother dressed up in a sheet!

scrub

To scrub is to clean something by rubbing it very hard with a brush and water. Mr Fussy scrubs his floor with a scrubbing brush every morning and every evening.

scrub

scruffy

Scruffy means untidy and dirty. Mr Messy was very scruffy until Mr Neat and Mr Tidy came to visit him.

sea

The sea is all the water that covers three-quarters of the earth's surface. At the seaside you can paddle or swim in the sea. Ships sail across the sea to different countries.

seal

seal

A seal is an animal that lives by the sea and sometimes in the sea. Seals have flippers instead of legs to help them swim. Baby seals are called pups and are covered in a thick, soft fur.

To seal means to stick down. You seal the edge of an envelope to keep it closed.

search

To search means to try and find something by looking very carefully for it. Mr Chatterbox searched his house for his shoes. But Mr Mischief had hidden them in the garden. Mr Chatterbox would never think of looking for them there.

season

A season is a particular time of the year. The year is divided into four seasons. Spring, summer, autumn and winter are seasons.

seat

A seat is something to sit on. Chairs and benches and stools are all seats.

second

Second means coming after the first. Mr Busy came second in the running race. Mr Rush finished first.

A second is also a very short length of time. There are 60 seconds in a minute. It takes only a second to wink your eye.

secret

A secret is something that is known to some people but not to others. When you are told a secret, you must keep it to yourself and not tell anyone else.

seed

A seed is the small part of a plant that will grow into a new plant.

seem

To seem means to appear to be. Mr Dizzy thought Mr Tall seemed shorter than usual. He hadn't noticed that Mr Tall was kneeling down!

selfish

Selfish means too interested in yourself and not thinking of other people. A selfish person doesn't usually help other people or share things with them.

sell

To sell is to exchange something for money. A butcher sells meat in his shop. He exchanges meat for money.

send

To send means to make something or someone go from one place to another. You can send a letter to your friend by posting it in a pillarbox. Mother sent Paul to the shops to buy some potatoes.

sensible

Sensible means having sense and not being foolish. It is sensible to carry an umbrella on a dark cloudy day, just in case it rains.

sentence

A sentence is a number of words put together so that they mean something. A sentence usually tells you something or asks a question. You start a sentence with a capital letter and put a full stop or a question mark at the end.

sentry

A sentry is a soldier who stands on guard outside an important place. Mr Uppity met a sentry at the King of the Goblins' palace.

sentry

separate

Separate means not together. Mr Silly and Mr Nonsense live in separate houses.

series

A series is a number of things of the same kind that come one after another. A television series is a number of programmes about the same people and shown at the same time each week or each day.

serious

Serious means not funny and not to be treated as a joke. The wizard was serious when he told Mr Mischief to stop playing tricks.

several

Several means quite a few. Mr Bounce had several presents for his birthday.

sew

To sew is to join pieces of cloth together with a needle and thread.

shadow

A shadow is the dark shape made on the ground or on a wall when someone or something is in front of a light. Mr Skinny's shadow is long and thin but Mr Small's shadow is small and round.

shadow

shake

To shake is to move something quickly from side to side or up and down. Mr Mean shook his money box to see how much money was inside.

To shake also means to tremble all over. Mr Jelly shakes when he is frightened.

shape

shape

The shape is the outer form of anything. The shape of Mr Strong's body is square. What shape is Mr Worry?

share

To share something is to give other people parts of it, or to let other people use it. Mr Happy cut his birthday cake into equal pieces and shared it with his friends.

sharp

Sharp means having a pointed end or an edge that cuts. It is easy to cut paper with sharp scissors. You need a sharp pencil to draw a fine line.

shed

A shed is a small wooden building for keeping things like tools and bicycles in. Many people have a shed in the garden or at the side of their house.

sheep

A sheep is an animal that has a woolly coat. Sheep are kept on farms. Sheep's wool is used to make warm clothes. Lamb and mutton come from sheep.

sheep

sheet

A sheet is a large piece of cloth that is used on a bed.

A sheet is also a piece of paper. You write a letter on a sheet of paper.

shelf

A shelf is a flat board fixed inside a cupboard or on a wall. You put things like books or food or cups on shelves.

shelf

shell

A shell is the hard cover that protects some animals such as tortoises and some kinds of sea creatures. The shells that you find on a beach once had creatures like mussels and whelks living inside them.

A shell is also the hard covering of an egg or a nut.

shelter

A shelter is a place where people or animals are protected in bad weather. When it rains, a bus shelter keeps people dry while they are waiting for a bus.

shine

To shine means to give off light. A torch shines in the dark. A street lamp shines at night so that people can see where to walk.

To shine also means to polish something to a mirror-like finish.

ship

A ship is a large boat that sails on the sea. Ships are used to carry people or goods across the sea.

shirt

A shirt is a piece of clothing. It has sleeves and a collar, and buttons up the front. Mr Muddle sometimes puts his shirt on back to front.

shiver

shiver

To shiver means to shake and tremble because you are cold or frightened. Mr Sneeze lives in Shivertown. Everyone there shivers all the time because it is so cold.

ship

shock

Shock is a sudden feeling of fear or a nasty surprise. The postman gave Mr Quiet a shock by banging very loudly on his door.

To shock someone is to make him feel very angry or upset.

shoe

You wear shoes on your feet. Shoes are made of leather or plastic and are sometimes fastened with shoelaces or straps and buckles.

shoot

To shoot means to fire a gun or an arrow and hit someone or something. The hunter shot two rabbits for his dinner.

To shoot also means to kick or aim a ball at a goal.

shoot

shop

A shop is a place where you can buy things. Everyone in Wobbletown knows when Mr Noisy is at the shops. He asks for things at the top of his voice!

short

Short means not long. "Cat" is a short word. It has only three letters in it.

Short also means the opposite of tall.

shoulder

Your shoulders join your arms to your body. Mr Small sat on Mr Robinson's shoulder when he drove into town.

shout

To shout is to call out very loudly. In Loudland everyone shouts instead of talking normally. And when they are angry, they shout even louder!

show

To show something means to let other people see it. Mr Uppity showed everyone his new watch.

To show also means to explain by doing something. I will show you how to make a model aeroplane.

A show is something entertaining. At a puppet show you can see a play performed by puppets. At a flower show you can see beautiful flowers.

shower

A shower is a light fall of rain.
A shower is also a kind of bath. When you have a shower, you stand upright and water is sprayed over you from above.

shriek

To shriek is to cry out sharply in a loud high voice. Mr Small shrieked when Mr Tickle tickled him.

shrill

Shrill means making a sharp, high sound. The children heard the shrill sound of the teacher's whistle in the playground.

shrink

To shrink means to get smaller. The King of the Goblins made Mr Uppity shrink whenever he was rude to people.

shrink

shut

To shut means to close up so that nothing can get in or out. You shut windows to keep the wind and rain out.
Shut also means not open. Most shops are shut on Sundays.

shy

A shy person is quiet and a bit frightened of other people. Mr Quiet is rather like that!

sick

Sick means ill. Mr Greedy sometimes feels rather sick after he has eaten too much.

side

A side is one of the edges or surfaces of something. A square has four sides. The teacher told the children to write on both sides of the paper.
A side is also the part that is on the left or the right but not in the middle. Mr Lazy has a table on one side of his bed, and a chair on the other side.

side

sideways

To move sideways is to move to the side instead of backwards or forwards. A crab walks sideways.

sigh

To sigh is to make a long, deep sound as you breathe out. People sigh when they are tired or upset or relieved. Peter sighed with relief when the bus came round the corner. He thought he had missed it.

sign

A sign gives you information or stands for something. There was a sign on the door of the shop saying "No Dogs Allowed".

To sign means to write your name at the bottom of a letter or on a form.

signal

A signal is something that warns you or tells you what to do. A red traffic light is a signal that tells drivers to stop.

silent

Silent means completely quiet. Mr Quiet likes the woods at night because they are silent. There is not a sound to be heard.

silly

Silly means not making sense. In Nonsenseland, birds fly backwards, which is really very silly.

Silly also means foolish. It is silly to eat too many cakes at a party, because you will only make yourself ill.

silver

Silver is a precious metal. It is greyish-white and shines when it is polished. Silver is used to make jewellery. Real silver cups and spoons are very expensive.

similar

Similar means nearly the same. Mr Happy and Mr Bounce are similar. Both are round and yellow. But Mr Bounce is smaller than Mr Happy and he wears a red hat.

simple

simple

Simple means easy. Mr Muddle cannot do even a simple job properly. Like hammering a nail into the wall!

since

Since means after or between a time in the past and now. Mr Bounce has stopped bouncing all over the place since he started wearing his new heavy boots.

sing

To sing is to make musical sounds with your voice. You sing a song. A choir is a group of people singing together.

single

Single means one on its own. There wasn't a single biscuit left on the plate after Mr Greedy had finished his tea. He had eaten them all!

sink

To sink means to drop down to the bottom of a liquid. A stone will sink if you throw it into a pond. But a piece of wood will float.

A sink is also a deep basin with taps. A kitchen sink is used for washing dishes in.

A stone will sink if you throw it into the water.

sip

To sip means to drink something by taking a little at a time. You have to sip hot tea. Otherwise you will burn your mouth.

size

The size of something is how big it is. You need to know what size your feet are when you buy new shoes.

skate

Skates are special shoes for rolling or sliding. They are not for walking. Ice skates have a metal blade on the bottom so that you can slide on ice. Roller skates have four small wheels to help you roll along the ground.

To skate means to move along on skates.

skeleton

A skeleton is the framework of bones inside a person or animal. We saw the skeleton of a dinosaur on show at the museum. The bones were enormous!

skin

Skin is the outer covering of the body of a person or animal. It helps to keep infection out of the body. The skin of most animals is covered with fur.

Skin is also the outer covering of fruit. Before you eat a banana, you have to take off the skin.

skinny

Skinny means very thin. Mr Skinny is so thin you can hardly see him when he turns sideways. He is not fat like Mr Greedy.

skip

To skip means to run lightly, hopping from one foot to the other. Sarah skipped down the road to meet her friend.

To skip also means to jump over a moving rope. When Mr Clumsy tried to skip, he got the rope tangled up in his feet and fell flat on his face!

skirt
A skirt is a part of a dress or a separate piece of clothing that hangs from the waist.

sky
The sky is the air above us. On a sunny day the sky is blue. But when it rains the sky is grey and full of clouds.

slam
To slam a door means to shut it with a loud bang. Mr Noisy never shuts doors quietly. He always slams them.

sledge
A sledge is a small light cart that runs over snow. It has flat pieces of metal or wood on the bottom instead of wheels. These help it to slide over snowy ground.

sledge

sleep
When you sleep you close your eyes and are not awake. You rest your mind and body completely. When you are tired, all you want to do is go to bed and sleep.

sleeve
Sleeves are the parts of clothing that cover your arms. Coats and shirts have sleeves. Long sleeves come right down to your wrist but short sleeves end above your elbow.

slice
A slice is a flat piece of something like bread or cheese or meat. Mr Greedy is cutting several slices of bread for his breakfast.

slice

slide
To slide means to move along smoothly. You can slide on something slippery, like ice or a newly polished floor.

A slide is for playing on. It has a smooth slope for sliding down and a ladder to climb back up to the top.

slip
To slip is to slide on something by accident. Mr Bump slips all over the place. Yesterday he slipped on the stairs. Today he slipped on a banana skin.

slipper

A slipper is a soft shoe that you wear indoors.

slippery

Slippery means very smooth and easy to slip on. Icy roads are slippery. So are rocks at the seaside covered with seaweed.

slit

A slit is a long narrow opening. Mr Nosey peeped through a slit in the fence.

slope

A slope is a piece of ground that is not level. Mr Funny parked his car on a slope and forgot to put the brake on. It rolled right down the hill!

slow

Slow means taking a long time. Mr Slow never does anything quickly. It takes him all morning to eat his breakfast!

slumber

To slumber is to sleep. Mr Lazy slumbers in Sleepyland all day long.

small

Small means not big. A mouse is a small animal. But Mr Small is even smaller than a mouse. He is so little you can hardly see him.

smart

Smart means neatly dressed. Linda looked very smart in her Brownie uniform.

smash

smash

To smash something is to break it into tiny pieces. Mr Bump smashed a window while he was carrying a ladder.

smell

You smell things with your nose. Roast chicken smells delicious!

smile

smile

You smile when you are happy or amused or being friendly. When you smile the ends of your mouth turn upwards. Mr Happy smiles a lot.

smoke

Smoke is a thick cloud that comes from something that is burning. A log fire smokes when it is burning. The smoke goes up the chimney.

smooth

Smooth means flat and even and not bumpy. Glass has a very smooth surface.

snail

A snail is a small animal that has a hard shell on its back. It has a soft body and moves along very slowly. Snails are found in water and on land.

snake

A snake is a reptile with a long thin body and no legs. It moves by wriggling along the ground. Some snakes have a poisonous bite and some have beautiful patterned bodies.

snap

To snap is to break something in two with a sudden sharp sound. Mr Jelly jumped in fright when a twig snapped under his foot.

snatch

To snatch is to grab something quickly.

sneeze

To sneeze is to make a sudden loud noise through your nose. You sneeze a lot when you have a cold. Mr Sneeze is always sneezing . A sneeze makes a sound like ATISHOO!

sneeze

sniff

To sniff is to take in a short breath through your nose. People sometimes sniff when they are crying or when they need a handkerchief. The dog sniffed at the biscuit to see if it smelt good enough to eat.

snore

To snore is to make a noisy breathing sound when you are asleep. When Mr Noisy snores, everyone for miles around can hear him!

snow

Snow is water in the air that has become frozen. It is soft and cold and white and falls from the sky in winter. When it snows, you can make snowballs and snowmen. Mr Snow loves the snow!

soak

To soak something is to make it very wet. Mr Clumsy was soaked when he fell into the swimming pool with all his clothes on.

soap

We use soap to wash ourselves and our clothes. Soap may be a solid lump, a powder or a liquid. When you mix it with water it makes a foam. Mr Messy doesn't like using soap!

sock

You put socks on your feet before you put your shoes on. Socks are made of wool, cotton or nylon.

soft

Soft means not hard or firm. A pillow is soft. So is a furry kitten. Mr Lazy likes to have a nice soft bed to lie on.

Soft also means quiet. It is the opposite of loud. Mr Quiet has a soft voice. You can hardly hear him speak.

soil

Soil is the soft brown surface of the land. Soil is also called earth. Plants are grown in soil. Mr Topsy Turvy dug a deep hole in the soil and planted a rose bush. Upside down, of course!

soldier

A soldier is a person who belongs to an army. Soldiers fight in wars. They wear uniform.

solemn

Solemn means serious. The children solemnly promised their father that they wouldn't play near the railway line.

solid

Solid means hard all the way through. A solid lump of wood is not hollow inside.

solve

To solve a puzzle or problem is to find the answer. Mr Muddle finally solved the mystery of his missing teapot. He had put it away in the oven by mistake!

somersault

When you turn a somersault you curl up in a ball and roll right over, forwards or backwards. Mr Tall's long legs get in the way when he tries to turn a somersault.

song

A song is a piece of music with words that you can sing.

soon

Soon means in the near future. Mr Chatterbox is going on holiday soon. He will be going away in a few days' time.

sore

Sore means painful. Mr Bounce got a sore head when he bounced up and hit the ceiling.

sorry

You feel sorry when you have done something to hurt or annoy someone else. You hope the person will forgive you.

sort

A sort is a kind or one of a group. Daffodils and daisies are different sorts of flowers.

To sort is to put things into groups of the same kind. Mr Small is sorting his knives, forks and spoons into separate piles so he can put them away.

sound

A sound is a noise or anything you can hear. A sound can be very quiet, like a pin falling on the floor, or very loud, like thunder.

soup

Soup is liquid food. It is made by cooking vegetables or meat in water or milk.

sour

Sour means having a sharp, unpleasant taste. Sour things are not sweet. Lemons are sour.

space

A space is a hole or a gap between things. When you are writing you leave a space between words. Otherwise your writing would be very hard to read.

Space is also the whole universe. Astronauts travel through space to the moon.

spade

A spade is a tool that is used for digging. Mr Sneeze took his bucket and spade with him when he went to the seaside.

spare

Spare means extra. Mr Worry keeps a spare front door key under his mat, in case he loses his other key.

sparkle

To sparkle is to shine with a bright light. Mr Busy's windows sparkled in the sunshine when he had finished cleaning them.

sparrow

A sparrow is a small brown bird. You often see sparrows in the garden.

speak

To speak is to say something. Nobody gets a chance to speak when Mr Chatterbox is around. He talks all the time!

special

Special means different from the rest, not ordinary. Mr Topsy Turvy has a rather special clock. It tells the time. Backwards!

special

speck

A speck is a very tiny bit. You will have to look very hard to find a speck of dust on Mr Fussy's shelves. He dusts them ten times a day!

speech

A speech is something special that is said in front of lots of people. You make a speech. Mr Chatterbox is good at making speeches. One of his speeches lasted all day and all night!

speed

Speed is how fast something or someone goes. Mr Rush moves along at great speed. He is always rushing somewhere and getting nowhere!

spell

To spell is to write or say the letters of a word in the right order.

A spell is a magic word or rhyme. The King of the Goblins put a spell on Mr Uppity. The spell made Mr Uppity shrink every time he was rude to anyone.

spend

To spend is to pay out money to buy something. I am going to spend my money on an ice cream.

To spend also means to do something for a time. Mr Daydream spends hours daydreaming.

spider

A spider is a small creature with eight legs. A spider spins a web and catches insects for food.

spill

To spill is to make things fall accidentally out of a container. Mr Wrong spills milk at breakfast time. Every day. All over the tablecloth!

spin

To spin is to go round and round very quickly.

To spin also means to make a thread from a mass of cotton or sheep's wool. If you spin wool into yarn you can knit or weave with it.

splendid

Splendid means wonderful or very fine. Peter's mother cooked us a splendid meal.

splinter

A splinter is a thin sharp piece of wood. Sarah got a splinter in her hand from the old garden gate.

split

To split is to break apart. Jim's trousers were too tight for him. They split the first time he sat down!

spoil

To spoil something is to damage it in some way. Mr Messy spoiled his carpet by spilling paint on it.

spoon

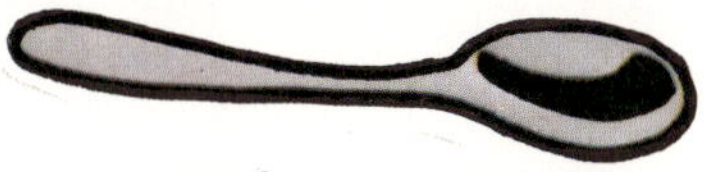

A spoon is a metal or wooden object with a handle and a round end that is shaped like a small bowl.

sport

A sport is a game or pastime mostly played outdoors. Swimming, football and athletics are sports, but chess is not.

spot

A spot is a particular place. This field looks like a good spot for a picnic.

A spot is also a small mark.

To spot means to catch sight of. Mr Nosey spotted an ant walking along his wall. He doesn't miss a thing!

spray

To spray is to wet something with tiny drops of liquid. Mr Fussy sprays his roses with water every day.

spread

To spread is to cover a wide area. Mr Tall spread the tablecloth on the lawn for a picnic tea.

spring

A spring is a coil of wire that makes something soft and bouncy. There are springs inside some armchairs and beds. This makes them more comfortable to rest on.

Spring is also one of the seasons of the year. It comes after winter and before summer. In spring plants begin to grow again.

To spring means to jump or leap.

sprinkle

To sprinkle is to scatter small bits or drops of something. Mr Muddle sprinkled sugar over his dinner instead of salt. It tasted awful!

spy

To spy is to watch people secretly. Mr Nosey spies on his neighbours by peeping through the curtains.

A person who spies on others is called a spy.

square

A square is a shape that has four sides and corners. The sides of a square are all the same length. Mr Strong is square. He is standing by a square house.

squash

To squash is to make something flat by pressing on it. Mr Muddle squashed his hat when he sat on it by mistake.

squeak

To squeak is to make a high, sharp sound. Bicycle wheels squeak if they need oiling.

squeeze

To squeeze is to press the sides of something together. When Mr Strong squeezes a tube of toothpaste, he presses so hard that all the toothpaste shoots out at once!

squirrel

A squirrel is a small mammal with a long, bushy tail. Squirrels live in trees and eat nuts. Most of them have grey fur.

stage

A stage is a raised platform at the front of a theatre or hall. People act a play on a stage so that the audience can see them clearly.

stain

A stain is a dirty mark that is difficult to wash out. Mr Messy's hands were covered with purple stains after he had been picking blackberries.

stair

A stair is a step. Stairs take you from one level in a building to another.

stair

stale

Stale means not fresh. Stale food is old and dried up and is not very nice to eat.

stammer

To stammer is to have difficulty in speaking. A person who stammers often says the first sound of a word several times before he can say the whole word.

stamp

stamp

To stamp is to put your foot down very heavily and make a noise. Mr Noisy stamps everywhere. Clump! Clump! Clump!

You stick a stamp on a letter or parcel to show that you have paid for it to be sent through the post.

stand

To stand is to be upright and not walking. The opposite of stand is sit. Your feet help you to keep your balance when you are standing.

star
A star is a bright object in space. We see stars as points of light in the sky at night. Some of them are millions of miles away.

A star shape has five points.

A star is also a famous person like an actor or a singer.

stare
To stare is to look hard at something for a long time. Everyone stared in amazement as Mr Impossible jumped over a house.

start
To start is to begin. Mr Slow arrived at the cinema. The film had already started, so he missed the beginning.

starve
To starve is to be without food for a long time.

station
A station is a place where trains or buses stop. Mr Lazy fell asleep on the train and got off at the wrong station.

stay
To stay is to remain in one place and not move away. Carol stayed on the beach all day.

To stay also means to visit a place and live there for a short time. Mr Skinny stayed with Mr Greedy for a few weeks to see if he could improve his appetite.

steady
Steady means firm and not moving. Mr Bump started to climb his ladder without making sure it was steady first. The ladder toppled over and so did Mr Bump!

steal
To steal is to take something that belongs to someone else and not to give it back. Robbers broke into the sweetshop and stole all the money.

steam
Steam is cloudy moisture. When a kettle of water boils, steam comes out of the spout.

steamroller
A steamroller is used for making roads flat. A steamroller has a large, heavy roller at the front and moves very slowly over a newly made road to make it smooth. Mr Slow once worked as a steamroller driver.

steep

steep

Steep means sloping very sharply uphill or downhill. Even Mr Rush was out of breath after running up the steep hill.

stem

A stem is a part of a plant. The flowers and leaves are attached to the stem. Most plants have a long thin stem that is green or brown.

stem

step

A step is one pace. You lift up your foot and put it down again somewhere else. You take steps when you are walking or dancing or climbing.

A step is also one stair in a staircase.

stern

A stern person is firm and strict, and looks rather cross.

The stern is also the back part of a ship.

stew

To stew is to cook food very slowly in water.

Stew is a meal made from stewed meat and vegetables.

stick

A stick is a long piece of wood. A dog likes to play with a stick and run after it.

A stick can also be a long thin piece of anything, shaped like a stick.

To stick is to fasten together with glue, tape or paste.

stiff

Stiff means hard and not easy to bend. New leather shoes sometimes feel very stiff until you have worn them for a while.

still

Still means quiet and not moving. Mr Busy never stands still for a second. He always has something to do.

Still also means up to this time. Do you still belong to the swimming club?

sting

To sting is to prick or stab the skin with poison. Bees sting with a sharp point at the end of their bodies.

To sting also means to have a sharp burning pain. When you put ointment on a cut it sometimes stings.

stir

To stir is to mix a liquid by moving a spoon round and round in it. Mr Muddle put a spoonful of sugar in his tea and stirred it with a pencil. Then he tried to write his shopping list with a spoon!

stitch

You make a stitch when you knit or sew. In sewing, stitches can fasten two pieces of material together. Knitted stitches are made with two knitting needles and wool. Hundreds of stitches knitted together make things like a jumper or a scarf.

stomach

Your stomach is the part of your body where your food goes after you have swallowed it.

stone

A stone is a very hard substance. Rocks are stone.

A stone is also the hard seed inside some fruits like peaches and plums.

stop

To stop is to finish moving. The taxi stopped at the traffic lights.

To stop also means to finish doing something. After five minutes of hard work in the garden, Mr Topsy Turvy stopped for a rest.

storm

A storm is very bad weather. In a storm there may be a strong wind and heavy rain, or thunder and lightning. The sea is very rough in a storm.

story

A story is a tale. Some stories are true but many are made up. You can read a story or tell a story. Mr Happy likes to read stories with a happy ending.

stupid

Stupid means foolish or not clever. The clever pig thought Mr Dizzy was stupid because he couldn't answer a simple question.

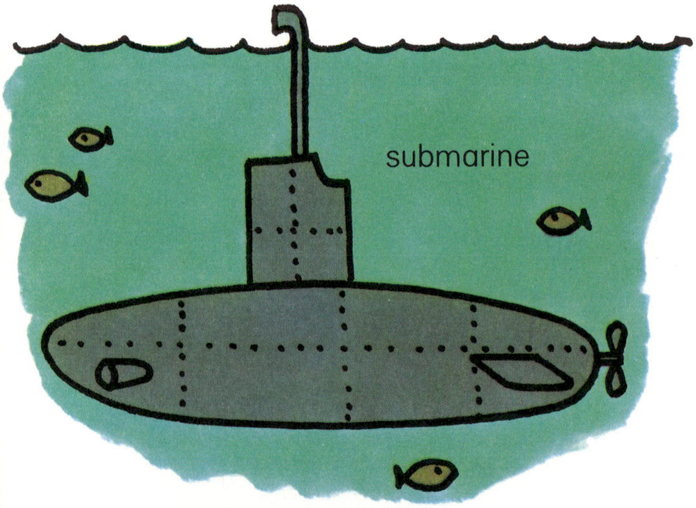

submarine

submarine

A submarine is a ship that can go under water. In wartime submarines carry torpedoes. They destroy enemy ships with them.

substance

A substance is what something is made of. Stone is a very hard substance and glue is a sticky, liquid substance.

succeed

To succeed is to do what you have set out to do. Mr Quiet succeeded in finding a job. He went to work in a library.

suck

To suck is to draw liquid into your mouth. You suck lemonade through a straw.

To suck also means to draw the flavour out of something in your mouth. If you suck a sweet it will last for a long time. But if you crunch it, it will soon be gone.

sudden

Sudden means happening quickly and not expected. Mr Happy had a shock when his chair suddenly collapsed beneath him. Mr Mischief had sawn through one of the legs!

sudden

sugar

Sugar is a food that is added to other foods and drink to make them sweeter. It comes from sugar cane or sugar beet plants. Sugar looks like very small grains of sand and can be white or brown.

suggest

To suggest is to give someone an idea. The doctor suggested to Mr Skinny that a holiday with Mr Greedy might help improve his appetite. Mr Skinny thought this was quite a sensible suggestion.

suit

To suit is to be right for. Mr Chatterbox thought his lovely new hat suited him very well. He thought it made him look very smart.

A suit is a set of clothes. A man's suit has a pair of trousers, a jacket and sometimes a waistcoat too.

suit

summer

Summer is a season of the year. It comes after spring. The summer is usually the hottest time of the year. Many people go on holiday in the summer.

sun

The sun is a very large, hot, bright star in the sky. The sun gives us light and heat and is seen during the day. Sometimes when the sun is very hot it makes your skin go red or brown.

supermarket

A supermarket is a very large shop that sells all kinds of food and goods. In a supermarket you put what you want in a trolley or a basket and pay for them at the checkout.

supper

Supper is the last meal of the day. Mr Silly has cornflakes on toast for his supper, with a cup of cold porridge. Ugh!

supper

support

To support is to hold up. The top of a table is supported by four legs. A swing is supported by chains or ropes fixed to a bar at the top.

suppose

To suppose is to think something will happen. I suppose it will start raining as soon as we set off for the seaside.

To be supposed to do something is to be expected to do it. You are supposed to talk quietly in the library.

sure

Sure means certain and having no doubt. Mr Sneeze was sure that it would snow again in Shivertown. And he was right!

surface

surface

The surface is the top or outside of something. The surface of the road was very bumpy.

surgery

A surgery is the room where a doctor, dentist or vet treats his patients.

surname

Your surname is your last name. Roger Hargreaves' surname is Hargreaves.

surprise

A surprise is something that you do not expect to happen. A surprise can be nice or unpleasant. Mr Greedy had an unpleasant surprise when he bit into the cake Mr Mischief had sent him. It was made of cotton wool and toothpaste!

surround

To surround something is to be on all sides of it. Mr Quiet's house is surrounded by trees.

surround

swan

A swan is a large water bird with white or black feathers. It has a long, curved neck and webbed feet. Swans can be found on rivers and lakes.

swan

sway

sway

To sway is to move slowly from side to side. The branches of the trees swayed gently in the breeze.

sweep

To sweep is to clean a floor using a brush or broom. The park keeper swept the leaves from the path.

A sweep is someone who cleans a chimney.

sweet

Sweet means not sour or salty. Sugar tastes sweet and so does food that has sugar in it, like chocolate and biscuits.

A sweet is something sweet that you suck or chew. Toffees and fruit drops are sweets.

swell

To swell is to grow bigger or louder than normal. A river swells when too much rain has fallen. The water rises and spills over the banks.

swim

To swim is to move through water using your arms and legs. Mr Rush can swim very fast indeed. He swims almost as fast as he can run.

swing

To swing is to move your body backwards and forwards by hanging on to something with your arms. Monkeys move from tree to tree by swinging through the branches.

A swing is a flat seat attached to an overhead frame or bar by chains or ropes. You sit on the seat and swing backwards and forwards. Most parks have swings.

switch

A switch is a button or lever used to turn electricity on or off. You switch a light on.

sword

A sword is a weapon with a long, sharp blade.

symbol

A symbol is a mark that stands for something. The symbol = means "equals" and the symbol + means "add".

sympathetic

When someone is sympathetic to you, he understands your problems and tries to help. Mr Happy is a very sympathetic person. He listened to Mr Miserable's problems and helped to cheer him up.

table

A table is a piece of furniture with a flat top and legs. You sit at the table to have your meals.

tadpole

A tadpole is a young frog. Tadpoles live in the water. They have a tail that begins to disappear as the legs and body grow.

tail

The tail of an animal is the end part of the back bone. Dogs wag their tails when they are happy. Monkeys use their tails to swing from tree to tree.

take

When you take something you pick it up with your hands. At the party, Mr Greedy took the biggest piece of cake.

To take means to carry. Some children take their lunch with them when they go to school. They take sandwiches.

Take also means doing something. You can take a dog for a walk or take a ride on a bus or take your place in a queue.

tale

A tale is a story that is usually not true. The tale of Mr Nonsense is about what he does in Nonsenseland.

talk

To talk means to speak and use words. Babies have to learn to talk. Mr Chatterbox has learnt to talk very well!

talkative

A talkative person talks a lot. Mr Snow is very talkative. He uses a lot of words to say very simple things.

tall

Tall means not short. Something that is tall goes high into the air. Mr Tall is very tall. So is a giraffe.

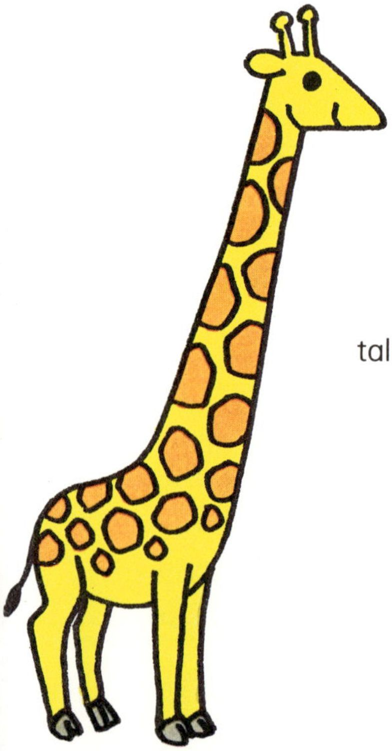

tall

tame

A tame animal is one that is not wild. Cats and dogs are tame animals. If you tame an animal you teach it to be friendly and not afraid of people.

tangle

To tangle is to twist things together so that they are difficult to sort out. Wool can get in a tangle while you are knitting.

tap

A tap is a knob that you turn to allow liquid or gas to flow. The bath has hot and cold water taps. You turn the taps on to fill the bath with water.

To tap means to knock something gently. You can tap your feet to music.

taste

When you taste something you put it in your mouth and find out what flavour it has. Sugar has a sweet taste. A lemon has a sour taste.

tasty

Tasty means having a nice flavour. Mr Busy can cook a tasty supper.

taxi

A taxi is a car with a driver that you pay to ride in.

taxi

tea

Tea is a drink made by pouring boiling water on to the dried leaves of the tea plant. You usually make tea in a teapot. You can put sugar and milk in tea.

Tea is also a meal that you have in the afternoon or evening.

teach

To teach is to help a person to learn. Mr Right taught Mr Wrong how to do things properly.

team

A team is a group of people who work or play together. A football team has eleven players.

tear

To tear is to pull apart. Mr Grumpy cannot stand books. He tears all the pages out instead of reading them.

tear

A tear is a drop of water that trickles out of your eye. When you cry you have tears in your eyes.

tease

To tease is to annoy someone in a playful way or to make fun of him. The clever elephant teased Mr Dizzy by asking him questions he knew he couldn't answer.

telephone

telephone

A telephone carries the sound of your voice by wires. It allows you to speak to another person a long way away. You dial a number on the telephone and speak into a part called the receiver. You put the receiver close to your ear to hear the other person talk.

television

You watch films and plays and all kinds of interesting programmes on television. The pictures you see on the screen are sent by signals that travel through the air. A television has to be plugged into an electricity supply to make it work.

tell

To tell someone something is to speak or write to him. When you write to a friend you tell him your news.

temper

Your temper is the way that you feel. When you are happy you are in a good temper. You may have a bad temper when you are angry. Mr Grumpy has a shocking temper.

temperature

Temperature is a measure of how hot or cold something is. You use a thermometer to measure temperature.

tempt

To tempt means to try and make someone do something. Mr Greedy is often tempted to eat more than he should.

tender

Tender means sore. If you fall over and graze your knee it will feel tender.

Tender also means kind and gentle.

tent

tent

A tent is a shelter made of cloth. It is held up by poles and tied with ropes to pegs in the ground. When you go camping you sleep in a tent.

term

A term is a period of time. A term usually means part of a school year. Autumn, spring and summer are school terms.

terrible

Something terrible is very bad and often frightening. Poor Mr Lazy had a terrible dream. He dreamt he had to work all day. How terrible!

terrified

If you are terrified you are very frightened. Most animals are terrified of fireworks.

test

test

To test something is to try it out. Mr Bounce tested his new heavy boots. He found that they stopped him from bouncing.

A test shows how well you can do something. Mr Wrong tried to do a spelling test. He couldn't spell one word right. Not one!

thank

To thank someone is to say how pleased you are for something he has done for you or given you. Mr Uppity never says "Thank you".

thaw

To thaw is to melt from being frozen. The ground is very wet when the snow begins to thaw.

theatre

A theatre is a special building where you can go to see plays and shows. A theatre has a stage for the actors and rows of seats for the audience.

thermometer

A thermometer tells you how hot someone or something is. It has a thin glass tube with liquid inside called mercury. The mercury moves up the tube until it reaches the right temperature.

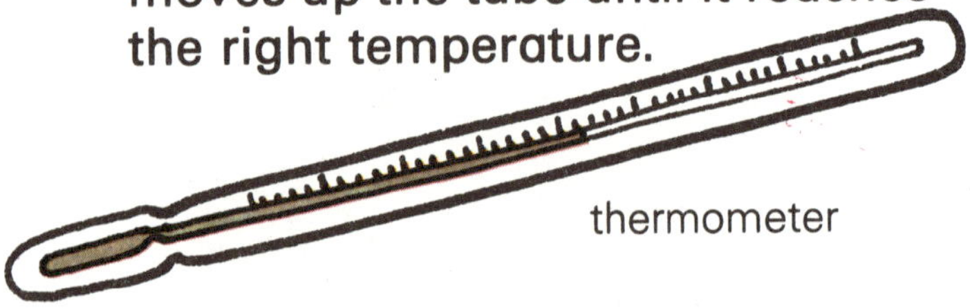

thermometer

thick

Something that is thick is wide or deep. It is not thin. There is always thick snow in Coldland where Mr Sneeze lives.

Thick also means very close together. The wood was so thick with trees, it was hard to walk between them.

thief

A thief is a person who steals.

thin

Thin means not fat or thick. Mr Skinny is so thin that if he turns sideways you can hardly see him at all.

think

When you think you use your mind. Mr Bounce tried to think of a way to stop bouncing. Then he thought of a good idea. He went to see the doctor.

thirsty

Thirsty means wanting a drink. Hot weather can make you very thirsty.

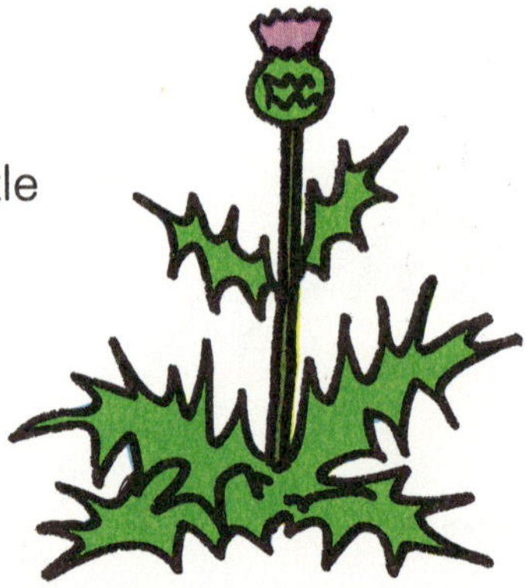

thistle

thistle

A thistle is a plant with prickly leaves. A thistle has a purple flower that turns into a white fluffy seed head.

threaten

To threaten is to say that you will do something unpleasant to someone. The wizard threatened to teach Mr Mischief a lesson if he was naughty again.

throat

Your throat is inside your neck. You swallow food down your throat. Mr Noisy got a sore throat when he shouted at the top of his voice.

through

If you go through something you go from one side or from one end to the other. When you are sewing you push a needle through the material, from the front to the back.

throw

To throw means to make something go through the air with your hand. Mr Strong is so strong he can throw a cannonball as far as you or I can throw a tennis ball.

throw

thumb

Your thumb is the shortest and thickest finger on your hand. Your thumb helps you to hold things.

thunder

Thunder is the loud noise that you hear during a storm. It comes after lightning. Mr Jelly is frightened of thunder. He hides under the bed during a thunderstorm.

ticket

A ticket is a piece of paper that you get when you pay to go on a train or a bus. You also buy a ticket when you go to the zoo or the cinema.

tickle

To tickle someone is to touch him gently. This feeling makes him laugh. Mr Tickle is always looking for someone to tickle with his extraordinarily long arms.

tidy

Tidy means neat and in order. You can make your bedroom tidy by putting everything away in cupboards and drawers. Mr Messy is not at all tidy.

tie

To tie means to make a knot, usually with string or rope. Mr Clumsy never bothers to tie his shoelaces.

A tie is a thin piece of material worn round the neck and fastened with a knot. You wear a tie with a shirt. Some children wear a special school tie.

tiger

A tiger is a fierce, wild animal that looks like a large cat. It has orange fur with black stripes, and it lives in the jungles of Asia.

tight

Tight means fitting closely together. It is difficult to untie a knot that has been tied tightly.

time

Time means the passing of minutes and hours and days. You tell the time by a clock. In Sleepyland everything goes so slowly, there is only time for four hours in each day!

tin

A tin is a metal container. Many foods are sold in tins. You open a tin of baked beans with a tin opener. Some tins have lids. These are used for storing things like biscuits and cakes.

tingle

To tingle is to have a prickling feeling. A cold bath makes you tingle all over.

tiny

Tiny means very small. Mr Small looks tiny beside Mr Tall. A mouse looks tiny beside an elephant.

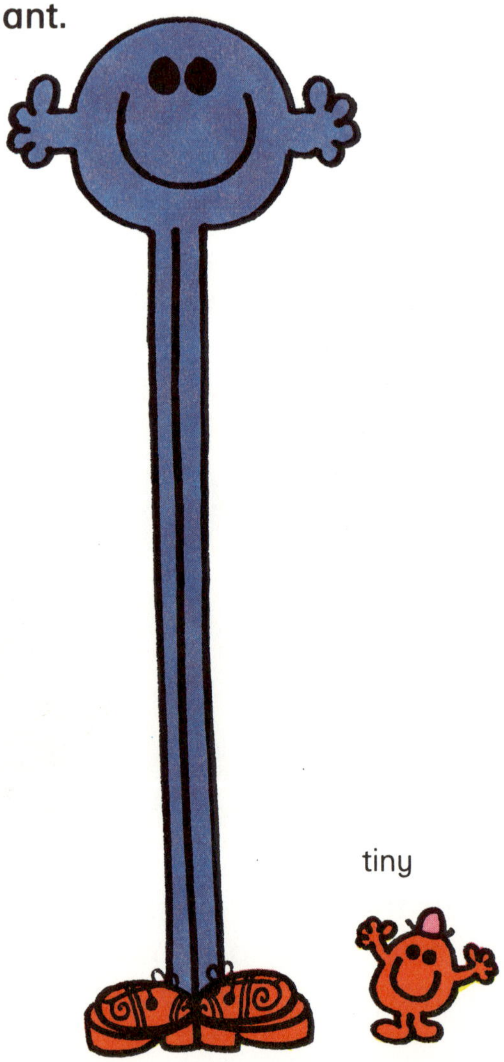

tiny

tip

The tip is the pointed end of something. A pencil has a sharp tip.

To tip means to upset or turn over. The chair tipped over when Mr Bump walked into it.

tiptoe

tiptoe

To tiptoe means to walk on your toes. When you tiptoe you can move about very quietly.

tired

When you are tired you feel sleepy and want to rest. Mr Lazy feels tired after walking to his front gate and back!

title

A title is the name of something such as a book or a film or a song. The title of a book often tells you what it is about.

toast

Toast is bread that has been made brown and crisp by heat. People often eat toast spread with butter and marmalade for breakfast. Toast can be cooked in a machine called a toaster.

toboggan

toboggan

A toboggan is a kind of sledge. A toboggan is usually made of wood with metal runners which slide over the snow or ice. Mr Silly and Mr Nonsense used a rowing boat for a toboggan.

today

Today means this day. If you finish your work today you can play tomorrow.

toe

A toe is a part of your foot. You have ten toes which help you to balance.

together

Together means with each other. Mr Bump and Mr Strong went for a walk together.

tomato

A tomato is a round fruit that is usually eaten as a vegetable. It has a red skin and is soft and juicy inside. You can eat a tomato raw or cooked.

tomorrow

Tomorrow means the day after today.

tongue

tongue

Your tongue is the part of your mouth that you use for licking and tasting. You also use your tongue when you are speaking.

tonight

Tonight means the night of this day. You had better watch out in case Mr Mischief is up to any of his tricks tonight!

too

Too means more than enough. When Mr Worry went for a walk he was worried that he might walk too far and be too tired to walk home.

Too also means as well as. When Mr Happy laughs everyone else laughs too.

tool

A tool is an instrument that helps us to do work. Carpenters use many different tools, such as hammers, nails and screwdrivers.

tooth

Each of the small white bones that grow out of your jaws is called a tooth. You use your teeth for biting and chewing.

toothpaste

Toothpaste is used to clean your teeth. You squeeze it on to your toothbrush from a tube.

top

The top is the highest part of something. Mr Nonsense built his house at the top of a tree.

topsy turvy

Topsy turvy means upside down and back to front. Mr Topsy Turvy gets his words the wrong way round when he talks. Everything about him is topsy turvy.

topsy turvy

torch

A torch is a small light that can be carried in the hand. An electric torch has a battery to make it work.

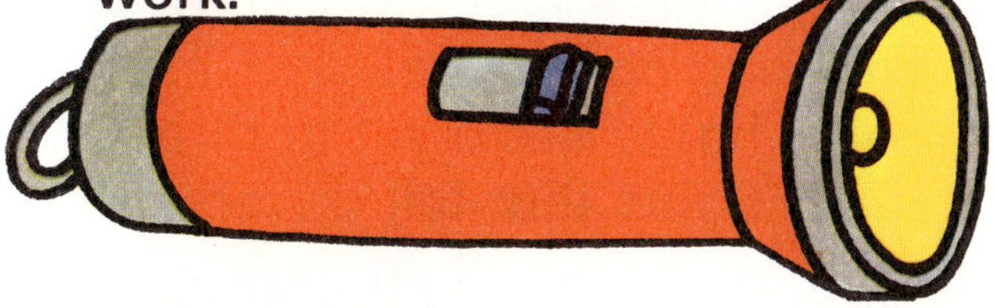

tortoise

A tortoise is a reptile that lives on land. A tortoise has a hard shell on its back. It can pull its head and legs inside the shell to sleep or protect itself from danger. A tortoise moves very slowly.

tortoise

totally

Totally means completely. If you agree totally with someone it means that you agree with everything that he says.

touch

To touch something is to feel it. You put your hand on something lightly when you touch it. Mr Robinson felt something touch his shoulder. It was Mr Small.

tough

Tough means very strong or hard to break or tear. Some meat can be tough and hard to bite.

towards

If you move towards something you move in the direction of it. Mr Noisy is walking towards his house.

towel

A towel is a piece of cloth that is used to dry wet things. You dry yourself on a towel after you have had a bath. Kitchen towels are sometimes made of paper.

town

A town is a collection of houses, shops and other buildings and all the people living there. A town is larger than a village and smaller than a city.

town

toy

A toy is something that you play with. Dolls and model cars are toys. Mr Snow helped Father Christmas to deliver his toys.

trace

When you trace something you put a piece of thin paper over it and go round the outline with a pencil. You can make an exact copy of something by tracing it.

track

A track is a set of marks left on the ground when a person, animal or vehicle has been over it. The tractor left a deep muddy track across the field.

A track is also a path or the rails on which a train runs.

tractor

A tractor is a vehicle that is used on a farm to pull heavy loads.

traffic

Traffic means everything that moves by road, sea and air. When there is too much traffic on the roads, there is a traffic jam and nobody can move.

Traffic lights are a set of three coloured lights that tell drivers when to stop and when to go.

train

A train is a vehicle that runs along a railway track. Trains are made up of a number of coaches or trucks pulled by an engine.

To train means to teach people or animals to do something. The farmer trained his dog to round up the sheep.

trample

To trample means to tread on and squash. A clumsy elephant walked into Mr Fussy's garden and trampled on his flowers!

transport

Transport is any vehicle that takes people or things from one place to another. Buses and trains are kinds of transport.

trap

To trap is to catch and hold something or somebody. The tide trapped the children in the cave. There was no way that they could escape until the tide went out.

A trap is something for catching animals.

travel

To travel means to go from one place to another. Mr Rush travels from one side of the country to the other. Fast!

tray

A tray is a flat piece of wood, tin or plastic that is used for carrying things. You can carry cups and saucers on a tray.

treacle

Treacle is a thick brown syrup made from sugar. You can use it to make treacle tart or treacle toffee. Mr Mischief filled Mr Funny's hat with sticky treacle. What a nasty trick!

tread

To tread means to put your foot down on something. Mr Small has to be careful when he goes out for a walk, in case someone treads on him.

treasure

Treasure is a collection of valuable things. The divers searched for hidden treasure in the wrecked ship.

treat

A treat is something that is very enjoyable and that doesn't often happen. We are having strawberries and cream for tea today for a special treat.

To treat means to behave towards someone in a certain way. If you treat your friends well, you are friendly and nice to them.

To treat also means to give medical attention. A doctor treats his patients and helps them to get well again.

tree

tree

A tree is a large plant with a thick wooden trunk, branches and leaves. Some trees lose their leaves in winter.

tremble

To tremble means to shake from cold or fright. The slightest thing makes Mr Jelly tremble. Even the sound of a twig breaking makes him shake like a jelly!

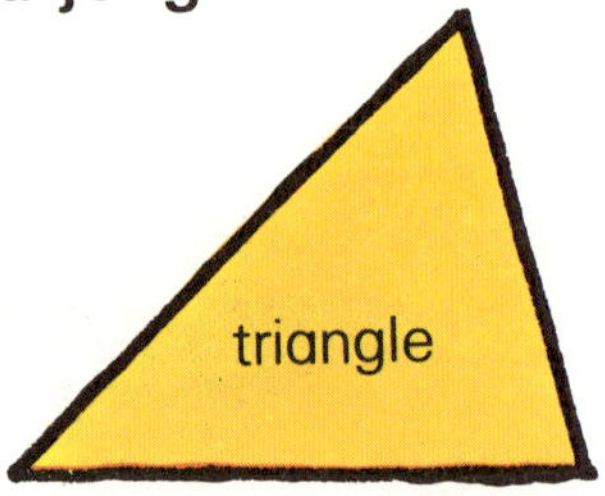

triangle

A triangle is a shape with three sides and three points.

A triangle is also a musical instrument. It is made of metal and makes a ringing sound when you strike it.

trick

A trick is a practical joke. Mr Mischief is always playing tricks on people.

A trick is also a clever act. It is very hard to know how a good magician does his tricks.

trifle

Trifle is a pudding made from sponge cake, fruit and custard. Mr Greedy loves trifle.

trifle

trim

To trim is to make something neat by cutting it a bit shorter. Mr Fussy trims his lawn every day. Fussy old fusspot!

trip

A trip is a journey or an outing or a short holiday. Jack went on a trip to Africa with Mr Daydream.

To trip means to stumble or fall over something. Mr Clumsy is always tripping over things. He even trips over his own feet!

trip

trouble

trouble

If you are in trouble it means that you have done something wrong or something unpleasant has happened to you. Mr Topsy Turvy was in trouble for putting all the books upside down on the shelves in the library!

trousers

Trousers are clothes that you wear on the lower part of your body. Trousers have separate parts to cover each leg.

true

If something is true it is correct and not false. It is not true to say that all birds can fly. But it is true that all birds have beaks or bills.

trumpet

A trumpet is a musical instrument made of brass. It is played by blowing through a mouth piece.

trunk

The trunk is the main part of a tree or a body. A tree trunk is covered with bark.

A trunk is a large wooden or metal box with a lid for carrying clothes.

A trunk is also the long nose of an elephant.

trust

To trust is to rely on someone to do something properly and honestly. The farmer trusts you to shut the gate when you leave the field.

truth

The truth is something that is true. Mr Mean is not telling the truth when he tells people that he is poor. He has lots of money hidden away.

try

To try means to do your best to do something. In a race, everyone tries to win.

tulip

A tulip is a plant with a cup-shaped flower and long thin leaves. A tulip grows from a bulb.

tulip

tumble

To tumble means to fall suddenly in a clumsy way. Mr Bump tumbled down the steps of the bank.

tune

A tune is a number of notes that make a piece of music. You can play a tune on a piano. Mr Busy likes songs that have a lively tune.

turkey

A turkey is a bird. Many people eat turkey for their Christmas dinner.

turn

A turn means a chance or a go. When you are playing a game you must wait until it is your turn.

To turn means to move round to face a different direction. The policeman turned round to see who was tickling him. It was Mr Tickle of course!

twig

twig

A twig is a very small branch of a tree or a bush. Some birds build their nests with twigs and grass.

twin

Twins are two children who are born to the same mother at the same time. Twins sometimes look very alike and it is hard to tell them apart.

twist

To twist means to turn round and round. To open a bottle of lemonade you must twist the lid until it comes off.

tyre

A tyre is the ring of rubber that goes round a wheel. It is usually filled with air.

turn

ugly

Ugly means unpleasant to look at and not beautiful. Monsters are very ugly creatures.

umbrella

You use an umbrella to keep you dry when it is raining. It has a handle and a round piece of cloth stretched over a metal frame.

umbrella

unconscious

When you are unconscious you lie still with your eyes closed and you don't know what is going on around you. When you faint you are unconscious. A heavy blow can also knock you unconscious.

underground

Underground means below the ground. Rabbits live underground in burrows. In some cities, trains run underground.

underline

To underline means to draw a line under a word or sentence to make it stand out.

underneath

Underneath means below or beneath. Mr Small lives in a small house underneath a daisy.

underneath

understand

To understand something is to know what it means. Mr Clever explained to Mr Dizzy how to make a pot of tea. But Mr Dizzy didn't understand. He boiled the tea leaves in a kettle!

universe

The universe is made up of all the planets and stars in space. Our world is only one very small part of the universe.

unless

Unless means except if. We will feed the ducks in the park today unless it rains.

until

Until means up to a certain time. Mr Mean never buys a new pair of shoes until his old ones are full of holes.

unusual

Unusual means strange or not common. It is very unusual for Mr Slow to be early for anything. He is usually very late!

uppity

An uppity person thinks he is more important than everyone else. Mr Uppity does not have many friends because he is so rude to everyone.

upright

Upright means standing straight up. You have to stand a bottle of milk upright once it is opened. Otherwise all the milk will spill.

upset

upset

To upset means to knock over. Mr Clumsy upset a pile of cans in the supermarket.

Upset means unhappy. Claire was upset when she heard that her grandmother was ill.

upstairs

Upstairs means one floor above. In many houses the bedrooms are upstairs. You have to go up the stairs to get to them.

urgent

If something is urgent it is very important and needs attention straight away. Mr Forgetful knew that he had an urgent message to give to Farmer Fields. But he couldn't remember what it was.

use

To use means to do something with. You use a pencil for writing. Mr Tickle uses his long arms to reach out and tickle people.

useful

Useful means being of use or helpful. Mr Clever has a very useful clock. As well as telling the time, it also says "Good morning", makes a cup of tea, and shows the date and what the weather will be like.

useful

useless

Useless means of no use at all. A pencil is useless to write with if the lead is broken.

usually

Usually means nearly all the time. Mr Happy is usually cheerful. But he was not very cheerful when Mr Mischief sawed the legs off his chair.

utterly

Utterly means completely. Mr Silly was utterly amazed to see Mr Impossible standing on no hands at the top of a lamp post!

valley

A valley is the low ground between two hills. A valley often has a stream or river running through it.

valuable

Valuable means worth a lot of money or very useful. Mr Uppity's watch is very valuable. It is made of gold.

van

A van is a covered vehicle that is used for carrying goods. The postman comes in a van when he brings a parcel. When you move house the furniture is put into a large van.

vanish

To vanish means to disappear suddenly. Mr Impossible can make things vanish just by waving his hand. He can even make himself vanish.

various

Various means several different kinds of. Mr Slow tried various jobs but he wasn't very good at them. Finally he got a job driving a steamroller.

vase

A vase is a container for holding flowers. Vases can be many different shapes and sizes.

vegetable

A vegetable is a plant that is grown for food. Cabbages, carrots, potatoes, cauliflowers and beans are all vegetables. And there are many more!

vehicle

A vehicle is used to take people or goods from one place to another. Cars, lorries and milk floats are all vehicles.

velvet

Velvet is a soft silky cloth. The threads stand up like short hairs. Velvet is used to make clothes and curtains and to cover furniture.

vicious

Vicious means fierce. Some wild animals are vicious when they attack.

victory

Victory means winning a competition or a battle. The local football team won a victory over the visiting team last Saturday.

view

A view is what you can see from a certain place. Mr Small has a nice view of Mr Robinson's garden from his window.

village

A village is a small collection of houses and other buildings and all the people that live there. A village is smaller than a town. Most villages are in the countryside and some are very old.

vinegar

Vinegar is a liquid with a sour taste. You put salt and vinegar on chips to make them more tasty.

violent

Violent means having great force or strength. A violent gust of wind blew the roof off the hen house.

visit

To visit means to call and see or stay with someone. Mr Skinny went to visit Mr Greedy to see if he could improve his appetite.

visitor

A visitor is a person who visits someone else. Mr Happy likes having visitors.

voice

Your voice is the sound that comes out of your mouth when you speak or sing. Mr Noisy has a very loud voice.

volunteer

To volunteer is to offer to do something without being asked. Mr Happy volunteered to help the farmer feed the pigs.

waist

Your waist is the middle part of your body, between your chest and your hips.

wait

To wait means to stay somewhere until something has happened or somebody has arrived. You wait for a bus at a bus stop.

walk

To walk means to move on foot. Mr Tall can walk a very long way in a very short time with his long legs.

wall

Walls are the upright sides of a building or a room. They are made from bricks or stones. A wall can also be a sort of fence. Mr Nosey likes looking round walls to see what is going on.

wall

wander

To wander means to walk about in no particular direction. Tramps wander round the countryside from town to town.

wander

war

A war is a battle between countries. Soldiers fight in a war.

wardrobe

A wardrobe is a piece of furniture that is like a tall cupboard. You keep your clothes in a wardrobe.

warm

Warm means fairly hot. You wash in warm water. Gloves keep your hands warm when the weather is cold.

warn

To warn is to tell someone about danger that might happen. A fire alarm warns people when there is a fire. The wizard warned Mr Mischief that if he did not behave himself he would be punished.

wash

To wash means to clean with water. Mrs Washer at the Tiddletown laundry washes clothes all day long.

wash

wasp

A wasp is a black and yellow insect that stings. A wasp makes a buzzing noise when it flies. Wasps can be a nuisance when you are trying to have a picnic.

waste

Waste means left over or finished with. You put waste paper and food in a dustbin.

To waste means to use carelessly. Mr Lazy wastes a lot of time sleeping all day long.

watch

To watch means to look at. Paul watched his father mend the car.

To watch out for means to keep a sharp look out for. Mr Nosey watched out for the postman on his birthday. He couldn't wait to open all his birthday cards.

A watch is a small clock that is usually worn on the wrist. Mr Forgetful keeps forgetting to wind his watch, so he never knows what the right time is.

water

Water is a clear liquid that has no taste or smell. Water falls as rain, and is found in rivers and lakes. The water that comes out of taps can be hot or cold.

wave

A wave is a moving ridge of water. When the sea is rough the waves are very big.

To wave means to move from side to side. When you wave goodbye to someone you move your hand to and fro.

wax

Wax is a hard substance that melts when it is hot. Candles and floor polish are made of wax. You can colour pictures with wax crayons.

way

A way is a path or direction. A signpost shows which way to go.

A way also means how you do something. Mr Topsy Turvy reads in a funny way. He reads a book upside down!

way

weak

Weak means not strong. When you are ill you feel weak and tired.

weapon

A weapon is used for fighting or for hunting. Guns and swords and knives are weapons.

wear

wear

To wear means to have clothes on your body. Mr Nonsense wears a green hat, blue gloves and blue and white shoes.

To wear out means to use something so much that it becomes thin or full of holes.

To wear out also means to make someone very tired. Mr Lazy was worn out after his long walk.

weather

Weather is what the air outside is like. The weather forecast tells you how hot or cold it will be and if it is going to rain or snow.

weave

weave

To weave is to make threads of wool or cotton into cloth. A special machine called a loom is used for weaving.

web

A web is a fine net woven by a spider. Spiders catch flies in their webs.

A web is also the skin that grows between the toes of water birds like ducks and swans.

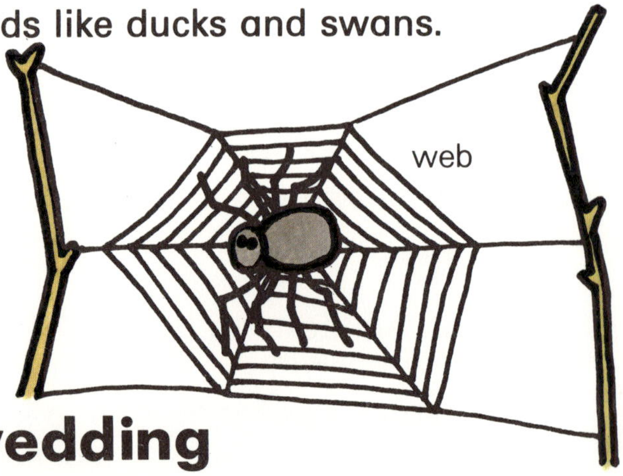

web

wedding

A wedding is when a man and a woman get married.

weed

A weed is a wild plant that grows where it is not wanted. Mr Fussy pulls up all the weeds in his garden as soon as they appear.

week

A week is seven days. The days of the week are Sunday, Monday, Tuesday, Wednesday, Thursday, Friday and Saturday. There are 52 weeks in a year. Saturday and Sunday are called the weekend.

weigh

To weigh means to find out how heavy something is. You can weigh things on scales. Mr Greedy weighs a lot because he is very fat.

weigh

welcome

To welcome means to greet someone in a friendly way. Mr Happy always welcomes his guests and offers them a cup of tea.

well

Well means in good health. When you are well, you feel good and full of energy.

Well also means in a good way. Mr Wrong didn't mend his chair very well. It broke again as soon as he sat down.

A well is a deep hole in the ground which may have water or oil in the bottom of it. Many years ago, people got all their water from wells because they had no taps in their houses.

well

wet

Wet means soaked with a liquid and not dry. Mr Grumpy's hat got wet when he left it outside in the rain.

whale

A whale is the largest mammal found in the sea. It has a tail like a fish and spouts water through a hole at the top of its back.

whale

wheel

wheel

A wheel is a perfectly round object that rolls along the ground. Wheels help vehicles to move along smoothly. Most cars have four wheels but bicycles have only two.

whisker

Whiskers are the stiff hairs that grow on men's faces and on some animals. A cat has long whiskers.

whisker

whisper

To whisper means to speak very quietly. You whisper to someone if you don't want other people to hear. Mr Quiet always speaks in a whisper.

whistle

To whistle is to make a high, thin sound by blowing through a small gap in your lips. Mr Happy whistled a happy tune as he walked to the shops.

A whistle is a small object that makes a shrill note when it is blown. The station master blows a whistle when the train is ready to go.

whistle

white

White is the colour of snow. Mr Slow has a white moustache.

whole

Whole means complete. Mr Small had a big lunch today. He ate one whole pea!

wicked

A wicked person is very bad. Mr Jelly read a story about a wicked witch who turned people into animals.

wide

Wide means stretching a long way from one side to the other. Mr Uppity has a very wide gate so he can drive his enormous limousine through it.

wild

Wild means living or growing naturally. Lions and tigers are wild animals. Dandelions are wild flowers.

win

To win is to be first or to do better than everyone else in a race or competition. Mr Silly won the Nonsense Cup for having the silliest idea of the year.

wind

The wind is moving air. A strong wind blows people's hats off and can even blow down trees.

wind

To wind means to turn something round and round. You wind a clock or a watch to keep it going. You wind wool into a ball.

window

A window is an opening in a wall of a building to let in light and air. Windows usually have glass in them. There are several broken windows in Mr Mean's house.

wing

A wing is the part of a bird's or an insect's body that is used for flying. Birds' wings are covered with feathers.

A wing is also the part of an aeroplane that sticks out on either side. The wings help to keep the aeroplane in the air.

wink

To wink is to shut one eye and open it again very quickly. People wink as a signal to someone else or to attract someone's attention. Mr Snow can wink his eye. Can you? Go on. Try it!

winter

Winter is the coldest season of the year. In winter most trees have no leaves, and there is often ice or snow on the roads.

wipe

To wipe is to dry or clean something by rubbing it with a cloth. When you have washed the dishes you wipe them with a tea towel to dry them.

wire

Wire is a thin thread of metal. Wires are used in electrical machines. When you plug in an iron, the electricity goes along the wires from the plug to the iron and makes the iron hot.

wise

Wise means knowing a lot and behaving in a sensible way. Mr Sneeze met a wise old wizard. He was so wise, he knew how to make the sun shine in Coldland.

wish

To wish for something is to want it very much and hope you can have it. Mr Dizzy wished that he could be clever.

witch

A witch is a woman who is supposed to make magic spells. You read about witches in fairy stories. They usually have a tall pointed hat and a black cat and fly on a broomstick.

wizard

A wizard is a man who is supposed to do magic. You read about wizards in fairy stories. A wizard uses a magic wand to do tricks. A wizard got hold of Mr Mischief by the nose when he tried to steal the wizard's magic wand.

wobble

wobble

Something that wobbles is very shaky and moves from side to side. A jelly wobbles. William couldn't balance on his bike. He wobbled from side to side and finally fell off!

wolf

A wolf is a wild animal that looks like a large dog. Wolves make a howling noise. Most of them are found in the forests and mountains of North America. Wolves hunt smaller animals for food.

wonder

To wonder is to want to know more about something. Mr Dizzy wondered what would happen if he put ice cubes in his tea. So he tried it. The ice cubes melted, and the tea went rather cold!

wonderful

Wonderful means very good or amazing or beautiful. Mr Tickle had a wonderful time in the park. He tickled everybody he could find!

wonderful

wood

Wood is the hard substance that we get from trees. The trunks and the branches are wood. Wood is used to make tables and chairs.

A wood is a place where a large number of trees grow together. A wood is like a small forest.

wool

Wool is the soft hair that grows on sheep. The wool is cut off the sheep and is then spun into thread. It is knitted to make jumpers or woven to make cloth.

word

A word is a group of letters or sounds that together say something we can understand. Several words are used to make a sentence. There are thousands of words in this dictionary!

work

To work is to do something that needs effort. Mr Busy works very hard. He cleans his house from top to bottom every day.

To work also means to have a job. Mr Small works with a man who writes children's books.

world

The world is the earth and everything on it and in the sky above it. Mr Daydream travels all over the world on his adventures.

worm

A worm is a small creature that crawls on the ground like a very small snake. A worm has a long thin body with no legs. Worms live in the soil. You often find them when you are digging the garden.

worry

To worry is to be anxious or bothered about something. Mr Worry is always worried about something. He even worries about having nothing to worry about!

worth

Worth means having the same value as. Mr Uppity's car is worth a lot of money.

Worth also means good enough for. When Mr Clumsy broke his teapot, he decided that it wasn't worth mending. It was already full of cracks and chips.

wrap

To wrap is to cover something all round with paper or cloth. Birthday presents are wrapped in colourful wrapping paper.

wreck

To wreck is to destroy something or break it up completely. The ship was wrecked when it crashed into some rocks.

wrist

Your wrist is the part of your body where your hand joins your arm. You wear a watch on your wrist.

write

To write is to put down words on paper with a pen or pencil so that people can read them. Mr Worry wrote a long list of all the things he had to worry about.

wrong

Wrong means not right. Mr Wrong wears his shoes on the wrong feet. He puts his left shoe on his right foot and his right shoe on his left foot. He never does anything right!

X

xylophone

A xylophone is a musical instrument. It has wooden bars arranged side by side. You play a xylophone by striking the bars with two special hammers.

Y

yacht

A yacht is a boat with a sail. The wind blows into the sail to push the yacht along.

yawn

To yawn is to open your mouth very wide and take a deep breath. You yawn because you are tired or bored. Mr Lazy always yawns when he wakes up because he is still tired.

year

A year is a period of time made up of 12 months or 52 weeks or 365 days. You have a birthday once a year.

yellow

Yellow is the colour of a banana. Daffodils have yellow flowers.

yesterday

Yesterday is the day before today.

yolk

The yolk is the yellow part of an egg.

young

Young means not old. A lamb is a young sheep. Mark is younger than David. Mark is six years old, but David is eight.

z

zebra

A zebra is an animal that has a white coat with black stripes. A zebra looks like a small horse.

zip

A zip is used to fasten the edges of clothes together. A zip has a clip that you move up and down to open and close the zip. Some dresses and trousers are fastened with a zip.

zoo

A zoo is a place where wild animals are kept so that people can see them. Many of the animals are in cages. Mr Funny went to the zoo. He saw an elephant, a lion, a bear and a giraffe.

A
MR FUNNY
B
MR IMPOSSIBLE
C
MR CHATTERBOX
MR FORGETFUL
MR TALL
MR NOISY
H I
J
MR HAPPY
MR NOSEY
MR STRONG
MR BUMP
MR LAZY
O
MR MISCHIEF
MR SNEEZE
MR FUSSY
U
V
W
MR CLUMSY
MR MESSY
MR SILLY
MR SKINNY